TEACH YOUR KIDS TO DRIVE IN 20 LESSONS

Mark Johnston

Spectrum Driving School Publishing

ISBN: 9798518098251

Cover design by: Art Painter
Library of Congress Control Number: 2018675309
Printed in the United States of America

CONTENTS

AUTHOR'S NOTE

The 20 Lessons contained in this book are reproduced in another of my titles:
'Teach Yourself to Drive in 20 Lessons'.

This book relates to driving on UK roads and taking a driving test in the UK.

The road can be a dangerous place. I hope you enjoy teaching your kids to drive, but please keep safety at the heart of everything you do.

TRANSCRIPT OF AUDIO SAMPLE

Welcome to the simplest way for you to help someone through their driving test, with or without employing a professional Driving Instructor. This book takes you from that first Sunday-morning drive around a deserted car park, all the way through to driving-test day, covering all the essential car control skills, road knowledge, and test manoeuvres along the way.

The beauty of it, is that you can just sit back with Junior, listen to a lesson, and then discuss it with him, adding in your tales of the road – your knowledge and experience – before finally taking him out to practice what's been discussed in that lesson. Then you can leave him to revise the lesson on here, just as many times as he likes.

Ah, yes, Junior. On here, that's what we'll call the person you're giving your time – and possibly trusting your precious car – to.

The lessons here have been developed by me over a 30 year career as a driving instructor, teaching almost two thousand pupils and covering over half-a-million driving instruction miles. I've also worked as a lorry driver, and my hobby is riding motorbikes, and both trucks and bikes have taken me all over the UK and Europe. I've also written extensively on the subject of driving, both online and for publication.

So these lessons are a result of a lifetime's road experience. But what these lessons *aren't* is a rehash of any official-sounding government driving book. So, errors and omissions, though hopefully few, are nonetheless accepted! But, as I said, that's where your knowledge and experience comes into the mix. We'll work together. I'll lay the foundations, you guys build on them.

In this audio, the individual lessons run from 5 minutes up to about half-an-hour, with the longer lessons broken down into two bite-sized chunks. The entire course runs for about five hours. And, yeah, I know, you might be concerned that Junior will think five hours sounds daunting, but during a course of professional lessons, an instructor would spend just as much time working through these same lessons, but with the two of them parked at the side of the road.

The actual *lessons* pupils are taken through, then – so the lessons in this book – are universal. So although every instructor might like to think of the way they teach as being unique, they all essentially cover the same basic lessons.

Okay, so the lessons instructors actually teach are covered in this book, but what about the practical aspects of a driving instructor's job? Because, I know what you're thinking, you're thinking that the driving test has changed massively since your day, that you're totally out-of-touch, and that all you'll really end up doing is passing on all those bad habits of yours.

But fear not... The first couple of chapters here are dedicated to teaching you how to get the best out of Junior – a crash-course in teaching you how to be an effective driving instructor.

So, yes, the test has evolved over the years. But that's the thing – it's *evolved* – a few subtle changes here-n-there, that's all. If you had to do another one today, no matter how long it's been since you did yours, you'd still recognise it. And the skills involved – the actual *driving* – well, that's the same as it's always been, you do it every day.

And those bad habits of yours? Well, if you really did have to retake your test today, how would you approach it, how would you actually drive? Would you have the radio blasting and a large coffee tucked in the cup holder? No, of course not. If your licence depended on it, you'd use a little bit of common sense and drive properly.

Properly, that's the key word here, that's how we're going to teach Junior to drive. The full official syllabus, taught systematically, one thing at a time, building up Junior's skills and knowledge in a structured way, everything he needs to know, all using simple everyday language.

A clutch, for example, essentially works like a kitchen tap. A tap controls the flow of water from the pipe to the sink – it can be dripping, or trickling, or gushing out – and a clutch controls the flow of power from the engine to the wheels in virtually the same way. So explaining clutch control to Junior by telling him to hold the clutch still, at the point where the power's just *trickling* through to the wheels, paints a picture he can understand.

So all those techniques and skills you mastered years ago, all that road knowledge, must now be broken down into its component parts. I'll do that for you. Everything you'll need. It's all in this book.

HOW TO BE A WEEKEND DRIVING INSTRUCTOR

Welcome to the simplest way for you to help someone through their driving test, with or without employing a professional Driving Instructor. This book takes you from that first Sunday-morning drive around a deserted car park, all the way through to driving-test day, covering all the essential car control skills, road knowledge, and test manoeuvres along the way.

The beauty of it, is that you can just sit back with Junior, listen to a lesson, and then discuss it with him, adding in your tales of the road – your knowledge and experience – before finally taking him out to practice what's been discussed in that lesson. Then you can leave him to revise the lesson on here, just as many times as he likes.

I said read or listen, because this book is available as audio, ebook or paperback, and many people like to listen to the lessons while following them along on one of the written formats.

The 20 lessons here have been developed by me over my thirty year career as a driving instructor. Over that time, I've also been a keen biker as well as a lorry driver, and I've also written extensively on the subject of driving, both online and for publication.

So these lessons are a result of my experience with the best-part of a couple of thousand driving test passes and a million driving instruction miles. But what these lessons *aren't* is a rehash of any official-sounding government driving books. So, errors and omissions, though hopefully few, are nonetheless excepted! But, as I said at the outset, that's where your knowledge and experience comes into the mix. We'll work together. I lay the foundations, you build on them.

Okay, so in this chapter I'm going to start by giving you an outline of the practical aspects of a driving instructor's job, and I'll be suggesting a couple of the *advantages* that you have over professional driving instructors, all before we get onto the actual lessons that you're going to be taking Junior through.

Ah, yes, Junior. On here, that's what we'll call the person you're teaching. Now, apologies if I've made all this sound very masculine, calling Examiners and other drivers *he*. It's not because of any bias, no, it's just for simplicity, and to avoid using the clumsy *he/she*.

Anyway, this first chapter is broken down into two parts. In the first part I'll discuss:

- What it takes to be a Driving Instructor
- Patience
- What Dual Controls are *really* for
- The luxury of time
- Law and Order

And then, in the second part, I'll run quickly through twenty-odd notes on things that I've learnt along the way.

Okay, let's get started with...

What It Takes To Be A Driving Instructor

As you know, getting your kids through the driving test costs a fortune. There's the driving licence, the theory and driving tests and, of course, the lessons. And we all like to save a few quid; so teaching them yourself maybe sounds like a good plan.

But, on the other hand, you might be thinking that the driving test has changed massively since your day, that you're totally out-of-touch. And maybe you think that if you did try to teach your kids, then all you'd end up doing is passing on out-of-date information and all those bad habits of yours. So perhaps you're thinking that although driving lessons are expensive, at least a professional instructor would have the knowledge and the experience to get your kids through the test. Then there are those all-important dual controls that instructors have fitted to their cars. They must come in handy at times!

And, yeah, okay – you've got me – some of that's true. But let's break things down:

Firstly, yes, the test has evolved over the years. But that's the thing – it's *evolved* – a few subtle changes here-n-there, that's all. If you had to do another one today, no matter how long it's been since you did yours, you'd still recognise it. And any changes there are to the test I'll cover in detail over this course of lessons. And the skills involved – the actual *driving* – well, that's the same as it's always been, you do it every day. And, as I've said, in this book there's everything you'll need for you to get those skills across to Junior.

Ah, but what about those bad habits of yours? Well, if you really did have to retake your driving test today, how would you approach it, how would you actually drive? Would you have the radio blasting your favourite tunes with a large coffee tucked in the cup holder, *zooming* along? No, of course you wouldn't. If your licence depended on it, you'd use a little bit of common sense and drive *properly.* It might take an hour-or-so of practice to get the hang of it all again, but you wouldn't have a problem passing.

Properly, that's the key word here, and between us, that's how we're going to teach Junior to drive. We're going to use your road knowledge and experience, and combine it with the lessons here. I'm going to break everything down into its component parts, teaching Junior everything he needs to know. The full official syllabus, taught in simple language, and taught *systematically*, one thing at a time, building up Junior's skills and knowledge in a structured way.

You see, to you, controlling a car's second nature, as natural as walking, say. But because driving seems so easy to you, you've probably not thought about the processes involved in it for a very long time.

I mean, imagine that an alien landed his flying saucer in your back garden one Sunday afternoon, and you went outside to offer greetings from planet Earth. There's the alien, floating about in mid air, and he asks you to explain the mechanics of walking... How do you stay upright? Why do you move your arms about? How come your feet things bend at the front?

Trying to explain how to drive's like that. The fine detail, the things *you* take for granted, need to be broken down and explained in simple, everyday language. There's no point getting technical. A clutch, for example, essentially works like a kitchen tap. A tap controls the flow of water from the pipe to the sink – it can be dripping, or trickling, or gushing out – and a clutch controls the flow of power from the engine to the wheels in virtually the same way. So explaining clutch control to Junior by telling him to hold the clutch still, at the point where the power's just *trickling* through to the wheels, paints a picture he can understand.

So all those techniques and skills you mastered years ago must now be broken down into step-by-step instructions. I'll do that for you. As I said, all you'll need to get those skills across to Junior are right here, in this book.

Ah, but didn't someone mention...

Patience

Most people assume all driving instructors were born with the patience of saints. But, well, no, not all! Some were, but others rely on a *professional* patience that comes from the experience of knowing just how long it takes to learn to drive. Try thinking of something Junior can do that you can't. C'mon, there must be something! Maybe the little clever-clogs plays guitar, or maybe he speaks French, or maybe he's just good at computer games. Whatever, how long would it take you to learn *that* particular skill, to be as good at it as he is? What, you think you just kinda strum a guitar and away you go? If you've never done it, it'll take you months, possibly even years, to get any kind of tune out of it.

Driving, then, isn't easy. Sure, some people pick it up quite quickly, but some don't. And if Junior has a problem with something, and he keeps making the same mistake, he isn't doing it to annoy you. The problem is either with the physical coordination needed for the technique – in which case you'll just have to bear with it for a while – or else he just doesn't understand what he's supposed to be doing – in which case you can try revising the lesson with him.

Either way, try not to lose that temper of yours! Keep your cool, and let Junior keep practising.

Now, what else? Ah, yes, the car. As I've said, driving instructors have dual controls fitted to their cars, so let's first talk about...

What Dual Controls Are Really For

And, yes, dual-controls are an advantage, there's no doubt, a fantastic safety feature. But in practice, driving instructors mainly use them more as a *time saving* feature. You see, dual controls allow driving instructors to put their pupils into situations that the pupil isn't yet completely ready to deal with, even with the instructor talking them through. So, you see, an instructor can have a quick chat with a promising new pupil, explaining the basics of, say, roundabouts, then take that promising new pupil to a roundabout on their first or second lesson, knowing that if the pupil becomes overwhelmed, he, the instructor, can step-in with the dual controls.

You won't have that luxury. But dual controls aren't a requirement for a driving test, and they're also not essential when you're teaching someone to drive. However, without them you really will need the patience of a saint, because *you* will need to be certain that you've built-up a solid enough foundation of car control skills with Junior before you allow him anywhere near his first roundabout.

Which brings us neatly onto the first *advantage* that you have over a driving instructor: you have…

The Luxury Of Time

Driving instructors have a weight on their shoulders – after all, as we've mentioned, driving lessons are expensive – so there's often an expectation for them to deliver a driving test pass within a certain number of lessons. Yet not all pupils progress at the same pace. A lucky few get through the test quicker than their parents expected but, unfortunately, many take a little bit longer and cost a little bit more. And instructors are generally limited to just one or two hours a week with a pupil. Hardly enough time to teach a new skill, reinforce it with practice, and then revise previous lessons.

But you don't have that problem. You *can* go over something *one more time.* You have time for that all-important revision of lessons already covered. And you have time to allow Junior to *just drive* on occasion, to not always feel like every minute needs to be spent preparing for the driving test. Every good instructor knows the importance of occasionally sitting back, keeping quiet, and allowing their pupil time to *just drive* for a while.

Another advantage you have over driving instructors is just how well you know Junior's personality. Driving instructors will have some pupils who are full of enthusiasm for each lesson, asking questions along the way, determined to get things right. While other pupils really can't be bothered, yawning like a well-fed lion the minute their instructor gets them to pull over to the side of the road and begins to explain something new to them. Now, instructors get good at spotting which kind of personality they're dealing with. But you don't have to – you already have a pretty good idea how Junior will respond.

So, maybe you know that Junior will be happy to go through the lessons with you, perhaps while sitting in the kitchen, enjoying that nice cup of tea. Or perhaps you know Junior to be the kinda guy who needs a bit more action – short sharp lessons with lots of driving.

Ah...but remember, this also means that Junior knows you! Maybe you're a bit speedy on occasion, maybe you've been known to let yourself down and indulge in a spot of *road rage* or whatever. Thing is, there's going to be a little bit of *do as I say, not do what I do* going on here. That's normal. Instructors are good drivers but they're not angels – and nor are Driving Examiners, for that matter! Thing is, you're going to be driving Junior between places on your lessons, especially in the early part of Junior's training, and you might even have to do the odd demonstration... Anyway, when you're called upon to drive, try to do it properly!

And do it legally. Because our next section is...

Law And Order

Junior's going to need his provisional driving licence – that's in his hand, not still in the post – before he's allowed out on the road. And he needs to be able to see, to be able to read a car number plate at twenty metres – which is about thirty good paces, to be on the safe side, using his glasses, or whatever, if necessary. And he needs to be insured for the car you're going to use. Junior's minimum age for driving is seventeen.

Your minimum age is twenty-one, and you need to also be in possession of a driving licence, but a full one, and you need to have had it for at least the past three years. And for this to work properly, so for you to be able to drive us from place-to-place, ideally you'll also be insured to drive the car.

Now, I assume you're planning on teaching Junior how to drive a manual car? If Junior passes his driving test in an automatic, then his full licence will restrict him to only driving automatics in the future. I realise automatics are becoming ever more popular, but this restriction will severely hamper Junior's driving life. Also, I appreciate circumstances might mean Junior can't physically drive a manual, so an automatic, possibly along with other driving aids, might be necessary. Either way, if you decide to use an automatic, this book is still for you – just ignore all the stuff about clutches and gear changes.

Then you're going to need 'L' plates and a stick on mirror-or-two. Four 'L' plates are a good idea. Legally you need one at the front and one at the back. But then one on each side, just behind the front seats – maybe in the rear passenger side-windows – are definitely worth having too. They mean that traffic approaching from either side of you will be aware that Junior's a learner – handy if he stalls, say, pulling out of a side road.

Mirrors? Well you'll need an additional rear-view mirror, one of those suction-cup ones, stuck up alongside the driver's rear-view mirror, for your use, and then for the Examiner's use on driving test day.

Door mirrors must be set up for the benefit of Junior, not for you. But it's a good idea to add an additional mirror to the passenger-side door-mirror for your use. This will obviously help keep you safe, especially when driving in lanes or heavy traffic, but it'll also help you to see what's going on, when Junior's practising his parking manoeuvres or whatever.

For the best possible view, a small additional mirror, clamped to the original door mirror, is best. But these do have a couple of problems. First, their metal jaws can scratch the paint on the original mirror's housing, and second, they're easy to lose – they'll get swiped off if Junior gets too close to a hedge.

The other option is a self-adhesive mirror, stuck directly to the original mirror's glass. These give you an okay view but without the problems of the clamped-on mirrors. However, the big problem with them is that once they're on *they're on*. If you fit one, then want to remove it, you might end up cracking the original mirror's glass.

But if you do go for one of the self-adhesive mirrors, first try fixing it to the main mirror with a bit of masking tape, to try it out in different positions. You want to have a decent view of what's going on, but without compromising Junior's view of the road. I normally go for the bottom right-hand-side of the passenger door mirror, an inch-or-so up from the bottom corner, but see what suits you.

Mobile phone and *due care and attention* laws are the same for you while you're supervising Junior as they are for when you're actually driving. So, no chatting on the phone or reading the Sunday papers as Junior bombs down to the shops.

So, insurance, 'L' plates and mirrors. After that it's all the usual legal requirements as for any car. Before his driving test, Junior will be asked to sign a declaration to confirm the car's legal for the road. Then the Examiner will take a quick look round the car – tyres, etc – before starting the test. If there are any issues, I'm afraid the test won't go ahead and you'll lose your fee.

And, talking of fees, you're not allowed to charge one! Not a problem if you're teaching your own kids, but if you're helping out and teaching, say, a neighbour's kid you're not allowed to charge for your services, and that includes *petrol money.*

Still with me? Good. Now we're going to run through 20-odd *tips* – just little observations and snippets of advice.

Things I've Learnt Along The Way...

Tip number 1: Try to enjoy the process. Teaching Junior will hopefully be a pleasure, not a chore. And this isn't *just* about saving money on lessons. Instructors know the amazing satisfaction of a job well-done gained by taking someone from their first nervous steps through to them passing the test. And, you never know, *you* might also learn something. You'll certainly come out of this experience as a more aware driver. There's nothing quite like answering a bunch of tricky questions, on any subject, to make you think things through, taking your understanding up a level.

2. Sometimes, especially in the first few lessons, it can feel like, no matter how many times you explain something to Junior, it's just not going in. Or, even though he's been practising something for what feels like ages, he's getting nowhere. In short, you think he's never going to get the hang of this driving lark. But, even though it might feel to you like he's not making any progress, he is. His brain has opened a new folder called *driving*, and, slowly-but-surely, it's downloading all these new skills, absorbing them. And tonight, as he sleeps, his brain will be figuring it all out, so that the next time he drives – *well, or maybe the time after that* – he'll nail it, *at last*. Then you can put his new found

skills down to your brilliant and patient instruction.

3. But, before Junior does get that new skill nailed, don't just stay on that one thing for hours-an-hours. This isn't *do or die.* Sometimes you'll simply have to give it up for today and go and do something else, something that Junior's more comfortable with. Come back to the problem issue next-time-out.

4. Don't judge Junior's driving on the way *you* drive now or even on the way you *think* you drove when you were a learner. Many of us have a rose-tinted view of our driving in our younger days. One day Junior will be every bit as good as you are now.

5. Don't take things for granted. I've had pupils come to me who've apparently been riding scooters on the road for months but still stop to look both ways at roundabouts. And then there's the one who'd always thought brake lights were just *like, random* – which explained why, when I was saying, *come on now, slow down when you see the car in front braking*, it didn't make any sense to him.

6. Buy yourself a notebook. In it, keep a record of your time devoted to Junior's progress. Also, in your new notebook, along with your hours of devotion, why not make a few notes on Junior's progress? Make notes on where you went and what you did, and the way Junior coped. Develop a grading system. Score him *one* if it was terrible, *two* if you had to offer constant instruction but it basically went okay, *three* when Junior gets by with a minimum of help, *four* when he manages something on his own, and, finally, *five* when he's really getting the hang of it. When you start to see lots of fours and fives, only then is it time for the driving test!

7. Don't be too precious about your car. The odd crunched gear or over-revved engine isn't really going to do any harm, is it? My driving school cars are rarely changed before 200k miles. Your wheels and tyres might get scuffed and your wipers might occasionally be dragged screeching across a bone dry windscreen.

But it won't last forever. Junior will improve. Patience, dear friend, patience!

8. Driving isn't a science, it's an art form. Yes, there are controls, but provided the car's essentially *under control*, and there's a degree of mechanical sympathy, does it really matter if Junior doesn't do things exactly the same as you do? Try to allow him to develop his own style. On test, Examiners don't expect perfection. Provided Junior keeps his cool, and stays in control of the car, the odd stalled engine, for example, is okay.

9. Different instructors will teach their pupils slightly different things in slightly different ways. There isn't just one way to teach someone to drive, so you can do it your way – with a little help from me, of course! When I first became an instructor a Senior Examiner in Luton once told me to *teach pupils to do what you do.* Good advice that I still follow to this day.

10. You must concentrate on what's going on the entire time you're supervising Junior. You know that sudden nervousness? The one that sets in when you realise you're going too fast for a situation? Doesn't happen to you nowadays very often, hopefully, but you know what I mean! Anyway, that same feeling can hit Junior at just 10mph, coming up behind another car in traffic. It's that sense of being overwhelmed – that there's just too much to cope with. And when it happens, you need to be there, maybe with your hand ready to haul on the handbrake, but mostly just with a word-or-two, enough to get Junior to the brake and the clutch, and to get things back under control.

11. Be positive. Listing Junior's faults will only depress the both of you. Okay, so, yes, noting and correcting faults is a crucial part of the process. But it needs to be done gently, and it's no more important than remembering to continually praise the progress that's being made.

12. But when you do feel the need to criticise, try to think before you act. Remember to keep things as positive as possible, espe-

cially in the first few lessons. Try saying, *well done, that was a much better gear change* rather than, *at last, you've managed to do something right.* And try not to jump in too quickly. Give Junior time to think. So, at junctions, for example, don't be too quick to growl, *come on, for goodness sake, what on earth are you waiting for?!* Because, as he dutifully follows your instructions, and drives off, you might just find that your view of the number seventeen bus was being obstructed by his head!

13. In the early stages of learning, Junior will only be able to cope with one instruction at a time. Multi-tasking is not an option. You must learn to break things down. You need to pause, and sometimes repeat yourself, to wait for *that* first instruction to be carried out, before continuing onto the next. You need to plan ahead, hundreds of metres, not tens of metres.

So those first gear changes, for example, will be: *We're going to change into second now. So, hand down to the gear lever, palm towards me. That's it. Now, clutch down…then come off the accelerator. Okay, now shift. Good. Now clutch up slowly and get back on the gas. Well done!*

You get the idea. Constant talking. Saying *where* to look. Saying what you're going to be doing next. But also saying what you're going to be doing *soon.* Asking questions. But then, if you don't get an answer, prompting for one. Only giving one instruction at a time. Waiting for Junior to act before moving onto the next one.

14. When Junior's driving, only use the word *right* as a direction. If you feel the need to start an instruction by breaking the silence, try using words like *okay* or *now* rather than *right.* I mean, imagine how confusing it would be if you kept saying, *right, at the end of the road, turn left.* And when he's driving, try to answer Junior's questions with either *yes* or *correct.* So if he asks, *should I use the left lane?* Say, *Yeah, that's correct.*

15. To give directions, Driving Examiner style, start by pointing

out whatever it is you want to bring to Junior's attention. So say, *at the end of the road* or *at the roundabout*. Next, give the actual direction. So, *at the end of the road, I'd like you to turn left,* or, *at the roundabout, I'd like you to turn left.* Finally, add-in some detail. So a full direction given on test will be something like: *at the roundabout, I'd like you to turn left, that's the first exit, signed London.*

16. But sometimes, even basic left and right directions can be too much for Junior to cope with, especially if things are getting a bit tricky. So if you find yourself getting too close to, say, parked cars, sometimes it's better to say, *move over your way a bit* rather than *move over to the right*. Even at junctions, at T-junctions especially, you might have instructed Junior to turn right, but he seems to be setting himself up to turn left, so you just add-in a little, *remember we're turning your way here,* rather than repeating to him that you're supposed to be turning right. If he's got his left and rights mixed up, repeating it isn't going to help.

This is all normal, and is part of the whole being overwhelmed thing. So, as usual, be patient, and work through it. It passes.

17. Focus on Junior's development and on aiming to make *safe progress*. That means driving safely and legally, driving at-or-around the speed limit, if possible. But *safe* progress is the goal. So, amber traffic lights, or that tiny gap at a roundabout – the gap you'd have got into easily – learn to let them go. Relax. You must concentrate on letting Junior do everything smoothly and safely.

Avoiding undue hesitation, which is driving test speak for *not hanging about*, will come with practice. Lots of practice, admittedly, but that's what you're here for! In the meantime, you must concentrate on doing things properly. So, if you're late leaving the house for the school run, you drive. Don't sit Junior in the driving seat but then try to hurry him along. A driving test involves driving safely and legally around a set route. Whether it takes thirty-five minutes or a few minutes longer isn't a consideration. On test, the idea is to drive like a chauffeur, not like you're late for work. There's no rush.

18. I know it's hard, but try not to worry too much about what other drivers are thinking. Sometimes Junior's going to make a mistake that another driver takes exception to. Happens all the time. All professional instructors are accomplished at the apologetic wave, given *without* eye contact but whilst *looking* busy supervising their pupil. If instructors reacted to every irate driver they'd be in more fights than Tyson Fury. So, again, try to let it go. Also, try not to stress Junior out just because *you're* conscious of holding someone up. Learners are slow – *thank goodness* – and everybody has to learn. So, again, a little wave – this time of thanks for being patient – and it keeps everybody calm.

19. As a pupil gets closer to their test, their instructor's comments often become a little more negative than they were in earlier lessons because of the way the driving test is marked. You see, a test is marked negatively, so an Examiner only marks down what a test candidate does wrong, not what they do right. In a driving test, points *don't* make prizes! The Examiner's score sheet starts clear – no faults – the assumption being that Junior will drive just fine.

So Junior doesn't actually have to *pass* his driving test, no, he just has to not *fail* it. So, approaching the test it's okay to say, *look, I don't think you're using your mirrors enough for the driving test,* or, *you pulled out too close to that red car on that last roundabout.* A driving test isn't like school – there are no 'B' grades, it's either 'A' or 'F'. It's either pass or fail. And a fail comes from just one serious mistake, so ironing-out Junior's faults is key to him getting a pass.

20. Keep revising. Don't assume that because you've covered a subject in detail, and Junior's done whatever-it-is just fine in the past – perhaps scoring a four or a five in your notebook – that your job here is done. No, go back and revise over and over again,

especially the basics. So as you work your way through each stage, making sure everything's understood and practiced, all the time you're also reinforcing previous lessons through revision. Just because Junior did a perfect hill start a couple of weeks ago, doesn't mean he'll do one again today!

So revision is also key to this process. And remember that not every drive has to be a new lesson. Some are just practice, and those family errands – popping out to the shops or doing the school run – are the best practice, and a great time to revise the basic skills. So you're always looking for a spare few minutes to do some simple left and right turns, and a couple of hill starts.

21. The Examiner begins the test by saying: *follow the road ahead, unless road signs direct you otherwise. If I want you to turn either left or right, I'll tell you in good time.* For Junior, this means his default position is, as your sat-nav would say, to *follow the course of the road.* So if Junior's approaching a standard traffic light junction, and the Examiner's keeping quiet, it isn't because the Examiner's forgotten to give directions. No, it's because he wants Junior to continue straight ahead.

The exception to this rule is at roundabouts. At roundabouts the Examiner will always give directions. So, on your lessons, especially as Junior gets closer to his test, try to use this system – to only give directions where necessary, to avoid constantly saying *go straight on.*

22. On test, Junior will be set the task of *Independent Driving.* This means following either direction signs or instructions from the Examiner's sat-nav. On test this lasts for about twenty minutes. To practice, at first, when Junior's getting the hang of things, you can just tell him to *head home.* But, as he gets closer to test, try to make it more challenging. Try saying something like, *follow the signs for London at the next three roundabouts.*

Oh, and if you're taking your test in Northern Ireland, then your Independent Drive will only be for a total of about ten minutes, and sat-navs aren't yet used there.

23. Route planning is a crucial part of your job here. Try to choose routes that suit Junior's level, but sometimes also ones that *demonstrate* a particular aspect of driving, something that you want to put across. So if you want to use a particular area to teach or practice a particular skill then, if necessary, drive Junior there – do the lesson – then drive him home again. And tell him the plan. Then try to stick to the plan.

When you're route planning, if possible, take the time to take a few photos that you can discuss with Junior before that day's drive. Maybe all the junctions you've done so far have *Give Way* lines but today you want to show him a *Stop* line junction. It's better if you can discuss the differences while looking at a photo of the actual junction you'll be using. Same with diagrams. A diagram explaining, say, a series of roundabouts, discussed with Junior before he drives round them for the first time, will help his understanding and calm his nerves.

Also, go to your local driving test centre and watch a few test candidates leaving with their Examiners – the Examiners wearing their fluorescent vests. You can find test start times online. Get to know which directions they head out in. What you're after is knowing what happens in those first all-important couple of minutes, the beginning being so important to any test. A good first impression. Looking for a good start, despite those frazzled nerves.

And it's the same for the return to the test centre at the end of the test. Look at the possible routes, at tricky turns and awkward junctions. Then try to work out a few places Examiners use on test, a few routes. But don't just follow some poor soul around their driving test. Imagine them, there they are, already nervous, and every time they look in their rear-view there's your big face looking right back at them. Instead, as you drive around your local area, watch out for driving school cars – especially if the guy in the passenger seat's in one of those vests – and start to piece together the area surrounding the Test Centre.

The actual drive on a driving test lasts around forty minutes, so take your area into consideration. Test Centres in rural areas might have routes going in a three-or-four mile radius, whereas a city centre test route will be a much shorter drive.

Finally, lesson 24. Trying your hand at real life *hazard perception*. Do you think you're a good driver? Well then, tell Junior...in the form of a running commentary while *you're* driving. Learner drivers tend to focus on what's happening right in front of them, tunnel vision, like a blinkered horse. So when you drive, talk out loud about what you're seeing and what you're planning on doing about it. The car pulling up...will a door open? The kids playing...will one step out? The new speed limit, the sign warning of a side road up ahead. Turn it into a game. How many things can you spot in one minute? Junior goes first, then you. Show him how much further you're looking ahead than him, how much quicker you're processing information.

And that's it, the end of your crash course on being a driving instructor. Hopefully you're feeling ready to put your knowledge and patience to the test. Hopefully you're feeling ready to get out on the road and use the lessons in this book. Each of the lessons builds on the last, so ideally do them in sequence. Listen to the lesson *then* drive. Don't play a lesson whilst Junior's driving. Then work on that lesson until Junior's comfortable with it – scoring 3s or 4s in your notebook – before moving on. Remember to revise. Remember to occasionally let Junior *just drive.* Think about places locally best suited to the lesson. Plan your route. Consider the time of day and the traffic. Drive Junior yourself from place-to-place, if necessary.

Now, you might feel confident taking Junior all the way to his driving test yourself, just using your wits and this book. Or you might decide to teach Junior alongside an Approved Driving

Instructor – an ADI – the three of you working together. This would give Junior the benefit of getting another perspective and another opinion. See how you feel.

Anyway, good luck. You're gonna need it.

(Just kidding!)

LESSON 1:
COCKPIT DRILL

In this lesson I'm going to be covering:

- Seat adjustment
- Mirror adjustment
- Securing the car

old

Okay, so The Cockpit Drill...sounds like you're going to be heading off to flight school – a bit like *Top Gun* – to be a fighter pilot, but no, it's not quite as exciting as that – a car's cockpit drill is simply making sure that you're sitting nice and comfortably, and also making sure that the car's safe, before starting the engine.

So, first thing's first, make sure the doors are properly closed. On your driving test, falling out would be a bad start! Once that's done, organise your...

NB: Don't die

Seat Adjustment

You've usually got three adjustments you can make on a driver's seat. On some cars these will be controlled electronically, on others you'll have to physically move the seat about. But let's assume yours are just plain old manual, so no fancy electrics.

Start with the seat's height. It's obviously handy to be able to see through the windscreen, but hopefully without your head rubbing against the roof. To do this, you might find it's easier to get back out of the car, to take your weight off the seat, before adjusting it up. Manual adjusters usually work like a kind of pump, so you literally pump the seat up. The handle to do this will usually be down between the base of your seat and the door. To set the seat height, unless you're really tall, start with the seat fully up, then, when you're back in the car, sitting comfortably, gently adjust the seat down, until it suits you.

Next, make sure you can reach the pedals comfortably. The lever to adjust the seat backwards and forwards is at the front of the seat, at the bottom near the floor, under one of your knees. Pull the lever to release the lock, then slide the seat forwards and backwards until you're able to press the clutch pedal – that's the one over to the left – all the way down, and to be able to hold it down comfortably, ideally with a slight bend at your knee. The lever is a simple locking mechanism, so it's usually best to take your foot off the clutch before you try to readjust the seat or else you might find yourself sliding backwards, and not able to reach the pedals at all. That's one of the reasons why it's not a good idea to attempt to adjust the seat while you're driving!

Then adjust the back of the seat for a comfortable reach to the steering wheel. There's usually a wheel or a lever down behind your hip that lets you move the back of the seat backwards and forwards. Then take hold of the steering wheel, imagining your hands to be at the ten-to-two position on a clock-face. Here you're looking for a slight bend at your elbows.

Finally, adjust the head restraint, commonly known as the head rest. The centre of the restraint should line up with your ears. There'll be a button by the head restraint that allows you adjust it up and down.

The steering wheel may also have a height adjustment. So if you're not comfortable holding the wheel, or if the top of the wheel obstructs your view through the windscreen, you can lower it slightly. To do that, there's usually a handle down beneath the wheel that you simply pull out to release the clamp that holds the wheel in position. You can then adjust the wheel up or down, then push the locking handle back into place.

Okay, now let's set the...

Mirror Adjustment

Start by setting-up the rear-view mirror. Firstly, notice that it has two fixed positions. If it's adjusted manually – again, some adjust electronically – then there's a lever behind the mirror that can be set to have the mirror pointing either up or down. You want it in the down position. This lever lets you flick your mirror glass up at night, if the car behind is dazzling you with its headlights. In this night-time up position you can still see following traffic but without the glare.

Now, take hold of the outside of the mirror, its frame, not the glass, so as to keep your mucky fingerprints off, then move it around gently until you can see as much as possible through the back window. Start by lining up the bottom edge of the mirror with the bottom edge of the back window, with your hair or your seat's head restraint just visible in the right-hand side of the mirror. Then make any fine adjustments from there.

Then set the side mirrors, the door mirrors. Again, they can be adjusted either manually or electronically, depending on your car. On the driver's side, set it so that you get the best possible view of the road, but with just a little bit of your own car in there too, just enough to give you some perspective between your car and any following traffic.

On the passenger side, do the same, except, when you've got it just right, tilt it down a fraction. You want it set so that you have a perfect view on that side of the car, but with just a hint of the kerb. It's really handy to have a slight view of the kerb or the white line when you're manoeuvring, you know, reverse parking or whatever.

Now, with your door mirrors set, take a moment to find a reference point in each mirror, so that you can adjust your mirrors into exactly the same position again the next time you drive the car. So what can you see in there? Maybe the door handle appears to be a couple of centimetres up from the bottom corner of the mirror? Anyway, having these reference points will really help when you're manoeuvring, because by making sure you always have the mirrors set-up the same, you'll always have the same reference points to use.

Finally, you'll probably find that you'll want to readjust the mirrors occasionally during your first few drives, as you get comfortable with your new personalised driving position. But, like the seat, don't make those adjustments while you're actually driving. It's safer to stop the car first.

Okay, so your mirrors are set. But now, take just a quick peek over your right shoulder, then back to your door mirror, and try to work out what you can't see in the mirror. Then do the same with your left shoulder. The stuff that you can't see is in your *blind spots*. Maybe there's someone's driveway there, or a parked car? Anyway, before moving away or changing lanes you'll need to glance – and it is just a quick glance – into one of the blind spots just before you commit yourself to steering in that direction. It's important because it is so easy to lose sight of another vehicle in there, and your Driving Examiner will expect to see you making those checks on your driving test.

Now put your seatbelt on.

So you now have your seat and mirrors adjusted, and your seatbelt on, so it's time to make sure the car's safe. This is called...

Securing The Car

And it simply means making sure the handbrake's on and the

gears are in neutral.

Again, some car's have a fancy electronic handbrake, but assuming yours doesn't, to check the handbrake's on, pull gently up on the lever. If you hear a click-or-two then the handbrake wasn't fully on. But try not to heave up on the lever as though you're lifting a heavy suitcase, just a gentle pressure should do.

Then, to check the car's in its neutral gear position, take the gear lever and move it to either one side or the other – towards or away from you – then release it. The stick should spring back into the middle. That springy bit that you can feel is neutral. Like the handbrake, there's no need to wrench the gear-stick from side to side. Be gentle with it.

Now, I'll obviously be talking about the gears in detail in coming lessons, but for now, it's enough for you to know that neutral is like zero gear – so when your car's in neutral, even if the engine's running, it won't try to drive away.

And that's it. So, to sum up, the cockpit drill includes:
- Doors
- Seat
- Mirrors
- Seat belt
- Handbrake and Neutral checks

And that's you, settled into your car, ready to go.

Don't slarve makes starving hardly ~~necessary~~ negligable

LESSON 2: THE CONTROLS

Here I'm going to be introducing you to some of your car's controls:

- Steering
- Handbrake
- Accelerator and Footbrake
- Clutch

The basic controls of a car haven't changed much in the past hundred years. But, of course, some car manufacturers haven't been able to leave the basics alone, so some cars might have a different type or position of handbrake, for example.

Anyway, the controls described in this lesson assume you're driving a normal car, one with an engine and a manual gearbox. Oh, and talking of gears, I'll not actually be discussing them just yet. We'll cover those in detail in Lesson 5, once you've learnt how to get the car moving.

Okay, so let's get started. Let's talk about the...

Steering

Look at your steering-wheel. Place your hands on the wheel at *ten-to-two*, like the hands on a clock-face, same as you did when adjusting the seat. This is the way you're expected to hold the wheel on your driving test, as it gives maximum control of the steering. So if a child ran out in front of you, and you needed to steer quickly, you'd pull the wheel down – giving you far more accurate control than having your hands sitting low and trying to push the wheel up. Also, if you were ever to bump your wheels down into a pothole, those two strong hands of yours, balanced on either side of the steering-wheel, will give you the best chance of keeping your car under control.

Now, some drivers, when it comes to steering, just press one hand into the rim of the steering-wheel and spin it round. While others, when, say, turning right, grip the wheel with their left hand then swing it over, past twelve o'clock to the three o'clock position. Both of these techniques, while they can work just fine, involve that swing over the top of the wheel, where one or both hands pass over the twelve o'clock position. This is known as *crossing your hands* and is marked against you as a fault on a driving test.

The correct steering-technique for a driving test, however, so the one we'll be using, is called *feeding the wheel.*

Now, turning a steering-wheel in a stationary car, even one with powered steering, isn't good for it. It strains everything from the steering-wheel right down to the front tyres, and is called *dry steering.* So when you're practising the movements of your hands around the wheel, don't actually turn the wheel unless the car's moving, just slide your hands around the outside of it. Or practice at home with a dinner plate. But that's an empty dinner plate, of course, not the one with your dinner on it!

Anyway, to get the feel of the way your hands work as you steer, take hold of the wheel, hands at ten-to-two, then slide both hands up towards twelve o'clock…then slide them both down towards six o'clock. And repeat. Try it for a moment. Slide both hands up to twelve, then both down to six. Twelve o'clock to six o'clock. Your hands always opposite one-another – one hand moving the wheel, the other simultaneously sliding round, following it – like a mirror image.

It takes practice. Most new drivers find this technique awkward at first. Stay with it. Keep practising. It might take a few goes, you may find that you'll need to do lots of laps of the car park, possibly even over several days, but you will get the hang of it, I promise.

Okay, so let's assume you've steered your car brilliantly around a corner, and now it's time to straighten up. Some drivers simply loosen their grip on the steering wheel, allowing it to slide back through their hands. But on your driving test your Examiner won't like that. What he wants to see is that you use that same feeding the wheel method to take the steering back off again.

I'll discuss the steering again in more detail, once we're ready to get the car moving, in Lesson 4, but now let's move onto the...

Handbrake

The handbrake's job is to hold the car still after you've stopped it with the footbrake. The handbrake's not designed to stop the car. However, if your footbrake ever failed – a scary thought – then pulling the handbrake on would stop you. But it wouldn't be a smooth stop. No, it'd be very abrupt, and it'd probably involve you skidding the back tyres. But, in an emergency, it'd be better than nothing!

There are three reasons why your handbrake's not as good at stopping the car as the footbrake. First, your car has four brakes – one on each wheel – and your footbrake is connected to all four of them, but your handbrake's only connected to the two at the back.

Secondly, with your footbrake, you can have a little or a lot of stopping power, depending on how hard you press the pedal down. But your handbrake doesn't have that level of control. It's just on or off. So when the handbrake's on, your rear wheels are locked-up tight, but when it's off, they're free to turn.

The final reason why it's better to stop with the footbrake is that it's connected to your car's ABS computer – the Anti-Lock Braking System – while your handbrake isn't. The ABS helps prevent you from skidding when you use the footbrake in an emergency or on a slippery road. The handbrake, though, as I said, isn't linked-up to the ABS, so if you were to pull it on while the car's moving, the back wheels will lock-up and the car will skid.

So, the footbrake's there to slow down and stop the car, and the handbrake's there to keep it still.

By the way, when a handbrake's on, we say that it's *set*, and when it's off we say that it's been *released*.

The handbrake has three jobs:
- Parking brake
- Hill brake
- Safety brake

So, in more detail, first, the handbrake's a *parking brake*. That means, if you plan on leaving the car you need to set the handbrake. If you forget, and you've parked on a hill…well, guess what'll happen.

Second, it's a *hill brake*. Say you've stopped at a red traffic light, facing uphill. You've got your footbrake on. Now, at last, a green light, so you need to get back on the accelerator to drive away again. Except, the moment you take your foot off the brake – if you haven't set the handbrake – you'll roll backwards, down the hill.

So, on a hill, stop with the footbrake, then set the handbrake to keep the car still. You can then move your foot from the brake to the accelerator, ready to go again, without having to worry about rolling backwards.

Finally, the handbrake's a *safety brake*. Say you're waiting to pull out of a petrol station, waiting for a bus to pass. Your feet are on the pedals, ready to go...but one of your feet slips and your car shoots forwards, completely out of control, right into the path of the bus. Nightmare. But if your handbrake's on, and you slip off a pedal, your car won't move. The handbrake will hold you still and your engine will stall, it'll conk out.

So, to be on the safe side, if you're waiting for something, say a bus to pass or a traffic light to change, wait with the handbrake on. On test, having the handbrake on whenever you're stationary for any more than even a few seconds, will make your Examiner just that little bit more relaxed, and we all want a relaxed Examiner! Marijuana).

Now, if you look at your handbrake, you'll see that it has a button on top of the lever. That button connects to a catch, a lock, on the ratchet system that keeps the handbrake on. To release the brake, pull the lever up slightly – you'll see that the button pops in a few millimetres – then hold the button in while you lower the lever all the way down. Then release the button.

Thing is, even though it only takes a second to release the handbrake, lots of new drivers try to rush it, letting go of the button before the lever's fully down. That means the brakes are still partially on. So try to take your time, and make sure the lever's all the way down before you let go of the button. Patienu

Then, to set the handbrake, again, use the button. Press it in, pull the lever up – and hold it up – until the button's released. Another common mistake is to pull the lever up but to then release the pressure on the lever before releasing the button, allowing the lever to drop down slightly. If you do that, the handbrake won't be fully on, so you could potentially roll on a hill.

Another common mistake, when putting the handbrake on, is not using the button at all, giving you that annoying clicking sound. That's called *ratchetting*. It doesn't really do any harm, but, yeah, it can be annoying. And, on test, try not to be annoying! Remember, we want your Examiner relaxed! So, hey, use the button!

Now I'm going to move down to your foot controls, starting with your right foot, so that's the...

Accelerator And Footbrake

The pedal over to the right is the accelerator, and the one in the middle is the brake. When you use these pedals, use them gently, with the ball of your foot, your heel on the floor. Get used to the feel of the pedals with the engine switched off. Feel the way the accelerator moves easily all the way down, while the footbrake has a firmer feel. Practice moving your right foot over from one pedal to the other, without looking down.

Driving Instructors often call the accelerator *the gas*. I suppose because we can say *gas* quicker than *accelerator*! But there's another reason. Calling it the accelerator might possibly make a new driver think it just makes the car go faster, to accelerate. But it's not. The gas works both ways. So, yes, press it down and the car will accelerate. But when you lift off the gas it slows down, it's an effect known as *engine braking*.

The use of engine braking is just about the best way to drive economically and smoothly. During engine braking, the system that pumps fuel into your engine shuts down, so you're not using any fuel – you're driving for free.

Imagine you're approaching a roundabout. You can see a few cars in your lane, queuing up. You're still a fair bit away from the roundabout, but at this point, lift off the gas pedal even though you're not going to brake just yet, to begin using engine braking. Immediately, you'll feel your car settle down. It stops using fuel and begins gently slowing itself down, giving the cars ahead of you more time to get moving, giving you more time to plan your approach to the roundabout.

Then, after maybe five or ten seconds of this nice, smooth engine-braking, you can use your footbrake – if necessary – for the final approach to the roundabout.

Looking ahead like this and easing off the gas when you can see that you're going to have to slow down for something, is known in driving books as *accelerator sense*, though a better name for it is probably common sense! The idea is that when you see a problem up ahead, ideally ease up, off the accelerator, to begin gently slowing down, *before* using the footbrake... Which is the middle pedal.

The footbrake connects to all four brakes, one on each wheel. The technique, here, is to try to use the footbrake *progressively*. Think of applying the footbrake over a scale of one to five – one being a gentle squeeze, five being pressing the brake down hard. Braking progressively is applying the brakes to a count of one...two...three. Then, just before stopping, easing progressively back up, off the brakes again: three...two...so that when you finally stop, the pressure on the footbrake is back at number one, barely squeezing the pedal at all.

Braking progressively like this means you'll stop nice-n-smoothly. But if you come to a stop with the footbrake pedal still down at number three, you'll stop abruptly, and everything on the back seat – possibly including your passengers – will fall on the floor.

Okay, so that's the gas and the footbrake. They're pretty straightforward, so it's easy to get your head round what they both do, but the...

Clutch

...is trickier, because sometimes when you press the clutch pedal down the car slows down, but other times it speeds up. Oh dear...

So let's try to clear up this contradiction. And to do that, let's start by picturing a bicycle. A bicycle works by the rider turning the pedals which turns the chain which turns the gears which, finally, turns the wheel. Then off goes our cyclist, merrily down the road. So the power from the bicycle's pedals is linked to the gears – then onto the back wheel – by the chain.

So a bicycle works by:

- Pedals
- Chain
- Gear
- Wheel

Now picture the workings of a car. There's an engine, which turns the clutch, which turns the gears, which turns the wheels.

So a car works by:

- Engine
- Clutch
- Gears
- Wheels

A car's clutch, then, does the same job as a bicycle's chain. It connects the power to the wheels, via the gears.

Okay, so let's go back to the bicycle, the rider happily pedalling along on a nice level country lane. Now, what happens when he stops pedalling? Does his bike stop dead in its tracks, throwing

him over the handlebars? Well, no, it doesn't stop, not immediately anyway. Instead it just kind of rolls along for a while, carried by momentum. It's called *freewheeling*.

And what happens when our freewheeling cyclist meets a hill? Well, uphill his bike will stop much sooner than on a level road, but downhill, especially if it's steep, his bike will speed up as it rolls all the way down to the bottom of the hill. A freewheeling bicycle, then, is controlled by the gradient: uphill it stops, downhill it speeds up.

So how does this relate to your car? Well, remember, at the start of this section I said that sometimes when you press the clutch pedal down your car stops but other times it speeds up? Well, that's because if you're driving along and you press the clutch down you're breaking the connection between the engine and the wheels – you're breaking the chain – and, just like a bicycle, your car's now freewheeling. And also, just like a bicycle, when your car's freewheeling it goes with the gradient – uphill it'll stop but downhill it'll speed up. Your car's simply rolling along – freewheeling – like a rollercoaster ride.

Oh, and another thing, when a car's freewheeling – just to confuse things – it's not called freewheeling. Oh no, that'd be far too easy! In a car it's called *coasting*.

So, when a car's coasting, it's simply rolling, so:
- Uphill it slows down
- Downhill it speeds up

Now, there are just three occasions when you need to press the clutch down. They are to:
- Coast
- Stop
- Change gear

Let's look at them in detail…

Number one, then, was to coast. Say you want your car to just gently roll up those last few metres to the end of a road. So, rather than having the engine drive you right up to the junction, for those last couple of car lengths, simply press the clutch down and coast up. Imagine, on a bicycle, how you'd stop pedalling and allow the bike to freewheel up to the junction. It's the same idea in your car.

Number two was to stop. Generally, to stop a car, you use the footbrake to slow down, then, just before you actually stop, you press the clutch down as well. So, to stop a car, you need two feet: one on the brake, one on the clutch.

But that doesn't mean the clutch is a kind of brake. Remember that going downhill the car will speed up when the clutch goes down, so you need to make sure that you have the car under control with the brake before the clutch goes down.

Finally, number three, was to press the clutch down to change gear. Er…self-explanatory, this one, I think!

Mistakes? Well, the main one is pressing the clutch down while you're braking. Braking, you'll remember, isn't on our list of the three occasions when you need the clutch. Stopping, though, is. And that's where the confusion lies. So, if you're braking, slowing down, you don't need the clutch. But if you then continue braking, right down to the point where you're about to stop, it's then that you press the clutch down.

Oh, and when you do press the clutch down, give it a good quick push, nice-n-positive. That way you'll get a clean break between the engine and the gears. There's no need to press the clutch down slowly.

So, we've discussed what happens when you press the clutch pedal down, and we've discussed the three occasions when you'll need to do it. But what about lifting the clutch pedal up, what happens then?

Well, when you lift the clutch pedal, you connect the engine to the wheels. When lifting the clutch, if possible, try to keep your heel on the floor. If you keep your heel grounded you lift the clutch by flexing your ankle and lifting your toes, allowing you the subtle movements needed for clutch control. But if you allow your heel to rise up, then you're trying to control the clutch by flexing your hip, which is a whole lot trickier!

Okay, so lifting the clutch pedal up. If your car's moving, and you've had the clutch down, say, for a gear change, then lift the clutch back up over a count of three: one...two...three.

Lifting the clutch gently in this way gives you a nice smooth transition from the clutch being down and the car coasting, to the clutch being back up and it being driven by the engine again. If you ease the clutch pedal back up, over that count of three, after a gear change, all you'll be aware of is a slight change to the sound of the engine, you won't actually feel anything. But if you lift the clutch abruptly – popping the clutch up – the car will shudder and lurch.

And what about using the clutch to get a stationary car moving? Picture a water tap. Say, a bathroom tap, allowing you to control the flow of water from the pipe into the sink. Turn the tap just one turn, nothing happens. But turn it a little more and you get a drip. A little more still, and you get a trickle. Until, finally, the tap is fully open and the water's gushing out.

Well your clutch is also a tap. But this one controls the flow of power from your engine to your gears – then onto the wheels – in the same way as the one in your bathroom controls the flow of water.

When the clutch pedal is held down, the tap is turned off, so no power flows. But then, as you lift the clutch pedal – like opening a tap – eventually you'll get a drip – a drip of power – making its way through to the wheels. Then, as you lift the clutch higher, the drip becomes a trickle until, when the pedal's all the way up, the power's pouring through, driving you along.

With your bathroom tap you have complete control over the flow of water. And it's the same idea with your clutch. When you're moving, say, out of a parking space, to keep things under control you can hold the clutch pedal still, keeping the power trickling through to the wheels, with your car barely moving. You have complete control over the flow of power. You have *clutch control.*

You see, your engine's a big bully – it wants to shove you forward – but your clutch keeps the bully in check, taming it. The engine *produces* the power but the clutch *controls* the power. And the clutch technique we use to give us that control – that clutch control – is called *Biting Point Control.*

The *Biting Point* on a clutch is the point where you've lifted the pedal – so opened the tap – just enough for a trickle of power to flow. Just enough to move the car. It's the foundation of every low-speed manoeuvre you'll ever do and we'll be discussing it a lot more in the coming lessons.

LESSON 3: MOVING AWAY AND STOPPING

This lesson includes a few sequences that you'll be using when actually driving, as well as some practical exercises. But remember, the exercises are not to be listened to while you're driving. Listen then drive!

Anyway, in this lesson I'll start by talking a bit more about the gas and the clutch, and about that all-important biting point. Then we'll move on to discussing:

- The simple secret to avoid ever stalling your engine
- Moving away on a level road
- Stalling
- Braking and stopping from higher speeds
- Moving away safely

But before we move forward, let's first cover some revision. In Lesson 1, when we discussed Cockpit Drill, and ensuring the car's secure, we mentioned that neutral is zero gear. If the car's in neutral – even if the engine's running – it won't drive off.

Also, remember that to check your car's in neutral, move the gear-stick sideways – towards or away from you – then just let it spring back to its central, neutral, position. The way that spring pulls the gear-stick into the centre is known as the gearbox bias. The bias in most modern gearboxes has the gear-stick sitting directly between third and fourth gears. So from neutral, if you simply push the gear-stick forward, you shift into third.

Just before starting your engine, always check the gear-stick – the spring – to make sure you're in neutral, and also check the handbrake's on.

So, now let's move forward, and talk in a little more detail about using the accelerator – the gas – when you're moving away. Picture a boat. Not a sailboat, but one with an engine. Maybe a speedboat. So the speedboat's engine turns a propeller. If you look over the back of the boat, there it is, spinning like crazy, foaming up the water.

Now, your car's engine does the same thing as the speedboat's engine, but, instead of a propeller, it spins a steel disc called a flywheel. The flywheel is about the same size as a dinner plate, and it's pretty heavy – you'd need two hands to carry one. Anyway, the main difference is that where the propeller may be just visible, dipping into the depths of the water, the flywheel's hidden away from view in the depths of the engine. So, a boat's engine spins a propeller, a car's engine spins a flywheel.

Okay does your car have a *tachometer*? It's a dial on the dashboard, also known as a *rev-counter*. The rev-counter's job is to let you know how fast the flywheel is spinning – how many revolutions of the flywheel there are in every minute – known as *Revs per Minute*, or RPM. And your engine spins really fast. Those single-digit numbers on the rev-counter have to be multiplied by a thousand, so when it shows '3' on the dial, your engine's spinning at 3000 times a minute – that's fifty times a second!

So, imagine you started your engine and let it run at tick-over, or idle. Let's say it idles at 800 RPM. Now, to produce enough power to actually move your car, you're going to have to set the gas. That involves bringing the RPM up to, say, 1500 by very gently pressing the accelerator, the gas pedal. At that point you'll hear the engine making a lively, humming sound.

Remember, though, that although the gas pedal produces the

power, it's the clutch pedal that controls the flow of that power to the wheels. So let's now delve a little deeper into understanding that control, and understanding the job of the clutch.

At the other end of the mechanism from your clutch pedal is a friction plate which, strangely enough, is known as a *clutch plate*. Its job is to grip – to *clutch* – onto the flywheel.

Imagine you're in your car, engine running, in gear, and you're holding the clutch pedal down. When the clutch is down, remember the tap is off, and, essentially, you're holding the friction plate away from the spinning flywheel – preventing the engine's power from flowing through to the wheels. Then, as you lift the clutch, like opening a tap, initially nothing happens – the friction plate just closes the gap between itself and the flywheel, taking up the free-play – so there's still no power getting through.

But then, finally, as the pedal slowly lifts – contact! Essentially, the friction plate and the flywheel meet. This contact is what, at the end of Lesson 2, we called the biting point, also known as *the bite*. It's the point where a drip of power's making its way to the wheels.

Now, at the bite, the sound of your engine changes, like a weight-lifter sucking in air preparing for a heavy lift. So, deep down in the engine, the friction plate has started to clutch onto the flywheel. But it hasn't fully gripped it yet, the bite is only the initial contact. But the bite is not the point where the bonnet lifts up or the back-end squats down. If your car reacts in that way, if it feels like it's desperately trying to move, the clutch pedal is up too high – above the bite – so squeeze it back down a touch.

This skill sounds simple, but keeping your clutch pedal nice-n-still when you're in a tight spot – keeping it just at that point where the car's moving under control – is the essence of low-speed car control.

This, then, is the breakdown for finding your clutch's biting point:

- Clutch in
- 1st gear
- Set the gas and keep it steady
- Find the bite
- Keep both feet still for five seconds…
- Then, clutch back down to the floor
- Come off the gas
- Keep your feet still
- Secure the car by moving the gear-stick back into neutral and making sure the handbrake's still on
- Relax your feet

So, preparing to move away by finding the clutch bite, goes:

- Clutch down
- 1st gear
- Set the gas
- Find the bite

Sometimes, though, finding the bite by simply listening to the sound of the engine can be tricky. The change in sound can be so subtle that it's difficult to hear. But if you get chance to practice this, get your Supervisor to park on a level area of a car park and try the following exercise:

- With the engine running, press the clutch down and shift into 1st gear
- Now, keep the clutch down and release the handbrake
- Then ease the clutch up very, very gently but **without using the gas**
- As you bring the clutch up to the bite the car will creep forward

- When you feel this movement, keep the clutch nice-n-still for a couple of seconds
- Then press the clutch back down again and the car will coast to a stop, perhaps with just a touch of footbrake

Now, it's really important to lift the clutch pedal slowly, then to keep it still again the moment you feel movement. That's the point you're looking for here. So:

- Clutch down
- 1st gear
- Handbrake released
- Ease clutch up until you feel movement
- Then…Clutch down
- Touch footbrake
- Keep both feet still
- Secure the car
- Relax your feet

Now let's move onto talking about what happens as you lift the clutch pedal up beyond the bite, and let's discuss a favourite lesson of mine…

The Simple Secret To Avoid Ever Stalling The Engine

So the secret to avoid stalling the engine, and also to moving away smoothly and under control, is to move away by lifting the clutch up above the biting point in two further stages, with a definite pause of a couple of seconds between those two stages.

So, the idea is to bring the clutch up gently to the bite. Then, when you're ready to drive away, to ease the clutch up again until you feel the car moving, but to then keep the clutch still for a couple of seconds, before easing it up again fully for the final stage.

Those couple of seconds between these final two stages give your engine chance to get the weight of the car moving.

Imagine a friend's car has broken down and he's asked you for a push. Would you run headlong at his car like an angry rhino, charging into it? Or would you get your body behind it, to gently move it, to ease it forward? Well your engine feels the same way. It wants to be given time to get the car's weight moving.

So, to recap, to move away smoothly: ease the clutch up to the bite, then up a little higher, until the car starts to move, but then keep that pedal still for a couple of seconds, before, finally, easing it all the way up.

I've already talked at length about thinking of the clutch as working like a tap. And I'm going to push the analogy even further now by using it to help describe the three stages over which you lift up the clutch pedal. The first stage, the bite, as you know, is a drip of power. Stage 2, when the car starts moving, is a trickle of power – enough to move you out of a parking space, say. And the third stage is when the clutch comes up completely, allowing the power to pour through to drive the wheels.

This next sequence is moving away and stopping using all three clutch stages:

- Clutch down
- First gear
- Set the gas
- Clutch Stage 1: find the clutch bite
- Now, release the handbrake…
- Clutch Stage 2: ease it up until the car moves
- Keep both feet still for a couple of seconds
- Clutch Stage 3: ease it up fully
- Let the car drive for a couple of car lengths…

- Then, clutch all the way down to begin coasting
- Gently use the footbrake to stop
- Keep both feet still
- Secure the car – that's handbrake and neutral
- Relax your feet

Let's tighten that sequence up a little:
- Clutch in
- First gear
- Set the gas
- Clutch 1: the bite
- Feet still
- Handbrake off
- Clutch 2: ease it up until you're moving
- Keep both feet still for a couple of seconds
- Clutch 3: ease it all the way up
- Drive for a bit…
- Then, clutch down
- Footbrake and stop
- Secure the car
- Relax

In these early stages you're trying to achieve four things:
- You're coordinating your feet to balance the gas and the bite
- You're feeling the way the clutch makes the car move as you ease it up over the three stages
- You're practising keeping your feet still for those crucial couple of seconds between each of the three stages
- You're getting used to coasting

Okay, those are the four things you're working on, but sometimes things don't go according to plan, and one of those occasions is…

Stalling

Stalling is when your engine cuts out accidentally. When you stall, the engine will fall silent, the rev-counter will drop to zero and various warning lights on your dashboard will light up. *Houston, we have a problem*! And that problem is most likely to happen when you're moving away, because, as you now know, it requires you to coordinate the gas, the clutch and the handbrake – so it does take a lot of practice.

But if you do stall, don't panic! Even the best of us stall occasionally. The most important thing is to make sure you keep your car under control, that you keep it still, and that it doesn't start rolling away from you. So you need a brake, preferably the handbrake. Then, either with the clutch pedal held down or with the gear-stick in neutral, restart the engine.

Remember, you will also stall if you don't press the clutch down just before stopping.

To stop in first gear, as discussed in the above sequences, press the clutch down first, *then* lift off the gas to get your right foot over to the brake. That way you'll slow down and stop nice-n-smooth.

But when you're…

Braking And Stopping From Higher Speeds

…the idea is to come off the gas first, to begin engine braking, then use the footbrake progressively, and then – when the car's slowing right down and you've got it nicely under control – to press the clutch down.

So, in first gear, press the clutch down, then come off the gas, and then brake. But in the higher gears, come off the gas first – to take advantage of engine braking – then brake, and then press the clutch down as you prepare to stop.

So, in first gear, press the clutch down first, before braking. But in the higher gears, you generally brake before the clutch goes down.

Okay, so far we've dealt with the physical act of controlling the car when moving away, but that's only half the story – the second part involves…

Moving Away Safely

To begin the next part of the moving away sequence, let's first think about looking in your rear-view mirror for any approaching traffic. The idea is to *give way* to that traffic coming up behind you. *Giving way* means not inconveniencing those drivers, not forcing them to either slow down for you or to have to steer around you.

Then, when you're clear in the rear-view mirror, indicate. The indicator here is to warn people in front of you that you're about to start driving towards them!

Then glance to your *blind spot* – that area alongside the car that the mirrors don't cover. If you're moving away from the left-hand kerb, check your right-hand blind-spot. If you're leaving the right-hand kerb, check your left-hand blind spot.

Finally, watch for any approaching traffic in your door mirror. The situation can change quickly, so you need to keep one eye in the mirror as you prepare to move away.

Then, once you've run through the safety procedure, it's time to release the handbrake, ease the clutch up over its second two stages, and drive away.

So the full moving away procedure has ten, yes, ten parts! And it goes like this:

- Clutch in
- 1st gear
- Set the gas
- Find the bite
- Mirror
- Signal
- Blind spot
- Door mirror
- Release the handbrake
- Clutch stages 2 and 3

And so the full procedure for moving away and stopping on a level road goes like this:

- Clutch in
- 1st gear
- Set the gas
- Clutch 1: find the bite
- Mirror
- Signal
- Blind spot
- Door mirror
- Clutch 2: up until you feel movement
- Keep your clutch still for a couple of seconds
- Clutch 3: all the way up
- Drive with the gas pedal for a couple of car lengths...
- Then, clutch down
- Footbrake and stop
- Secure the car

- Relax

So it's two feet to move the car and two feet to stop it again! Notice that simply taking your foot off the gas doesn't stop you. It slows you down, yes, but to stop the car you need to press the clutch down and brake, otherwise you'll just keep on going!

Practice, practice, practice. This stuff, as I keep on saying, is the foundation of everything you'll ever do in the car.

Don't rush onto the next lesson until you've got this one down. Moving away and stopping is such an important part of your driving test. Your Examiner will get you to pull over and move away again several times. So come back here, and revise this lesson, the night before your test!

LESSON 4: STEERING

Now that you can start and stop the car, it's time to find yourself a huge empty space to try your hand – well, both hands, hopefully! – at steering. An airport runway would be nice, but you're probably going to have to make do with a quiet, early-morning car park.

Steering takes priority over the other hand controls. The last thing you want, halfway round a corner, is to take your focus off the steering and move your concentration on to, say, the gears or the indicators. Do the steering first.

As I've already mentioned, when driving, have your hands on the wheel at roughly a ten-to-two position, to give you quick accurate steering and a good firm grip on the wheel. Also, remember that the steering technique you'll be using as you build towards your driving test is called feeding the wheel. This is where you keep both hands on their own side of the wheel, your hands opposite one-another, working between the top of the wheel – twelve o'clock – and the bottom of the wheel – six o'clock. Then, once you've finished the turn, use the same technique to straighten up again.

So, steering to the right, move your right hand up towards the twelve o'clock position, grip the wheel and pull it down. At the same time, slide your left hand down the other side of the wheel, so that both hands meet at six o'clock. Then, from there, grip the wheel with your left hand and push the wheel up, this time with your right hand sliding up the wheel, until both hands meet at twelve.

To turn left it's the opposite. Start by reaching up slightly with your left hand, then grip the wheel and pull it down, while at the same time sliding your right hand down, until they meet at six.

Before practising, maybe get your Supervisor to demonstrate a couple of things for you. Well three things, actually! Firstly, that the area you have to work in is big enough. From your starting position, you want to be able to steer to *full lock* – that's the point where the steering wheel won't turn any further, which on most cars is about one-and-a-half full turns of the wheel – and have enough room for the car to be able to turn all the way back on it-self, so that you're facing back in the opposite direction.

The idea is to be able to move away in a straight line and then steer fully, say, to the right, to come all the way back round and straighten up again. Then drive along again for a bit, before steering full-right again to bring you back round to where you started.

The trick here is to get the steering on nice-n-quickly, but then be a bit more relaxed as you take it off again.

The second thing you want your Supervisor to demonstrate is the steering technique that you'll be using. Now, this might be easier said than done, it might be that your Supervisor hasn't used this technique in years, in which case you can sit back and enjoy watching him tying himself in knots! But do watch – care-fully – because as you watch him coming to terms with the tech-nique it'll help you pick it up too.

The third thing that you'll want to see demonstrated is that, once it's moving, with the clutch pedal up, even if you don't touch the gas, the car will usually just keep on going. This means that once the car's moving, you'll be able to focus on your steer-ing technique without having to control the gas pedal.

Okay, so the demonstration we'd like to see from your Supervisor is the car moving away and then settling into the speed that it'll do on tick-over, just pulling itself slowly along without using the gas pedal. Then you want to see that you have plenty of room for the steering practice I described – so, essentially, driving around the car park in a big oval shape.

Notice that, especially in a straight line, you don't really steer the car with your hands, you steer it with your eyes – the car goes where you look. After all, you don't look at the handlebars when you're riding your bike, do you? No, you look where you're going. It's the same here.

Also note that the faster you go the more responsive your steering becomes. At 1st gear speeds you'll need to turn the wheel a lot to get the car to turn, but as you go faster the car steers with just the slightest movement of the wheel.

So, on the open road, at higher speeds, look well ahead, and look where you want to go. Try not to look down at the road right in front of you. That'd be like walking along the High Street staring down at your feet.

In Lesson 2, I mentioned dry steering – turning the wheel while stationary – and said it can lead to excessive wear-n-tear on your car's steering. But there's another reason to avoid dry-steering. If you turn the wheel while stationary at, say, a junction, then you'll lose track of where you'll end up going when you do finally drive off. So, turning left, leaving a side road, for example, if you turn the wheel while you're waiting for a gap in traffic, when you do finally get chance to move you're likely to bump straight into the kerb, because you'll have steered in too much.

And finally, note that when you're steering sharply at low speed the back of your car doesn't exactly follow the front. No, your back wheels take a short cut! Have you ever noticed the way a lorry driver swings his truck around a corner? When turning left at traffic lights, the front of the truck seems to go miles forward before the driver turns, yet the truck's back wheels barely miss the kerb.

Well, your car does the same thing, though not quite as dramatically as that huge truck. So, when you're coming forwards out of a space in a busy car park, you need to get at least half of your car out of the space before turning the wheel, otherwise the back of your car will scrape the car alongside you. Nightmare!

Anyway, now it's time for you to swap places with your Supervisor and try your hands at some steering practice. This is the exercise you're going to be doing:

- Clutch in
- 1st gear
- Set the gas
- Find the bite
- Mirror
- Signal
- Blind spot
- Door mirror
- Handbrake off
- Clutch 2: up until you move
- Keep the clutch still for a few seconds
- Clutch 3: pedal up fully
- Drive with the gas for a bit…
- But then off the gas, and let the car move on tick-over
- Now, steer round to the right, or left, until you turn all the way around and face back up the car park
- Remember, try to put the steering on quickly, then take it off again slowly
- Straighten up
- Drive along with the gas for a bit
- Then off the gas again and let the engine settle back

down to tick-over
- Steer fully back round to the right, or left, again
- Straighten up
- Drive back to the start position
- Clutch down
- Footbrake
- Stop
- Secure the car – handbrake and neutral
- Relax

And again, lots of practice! You must be able to comfortably move away, steer and stop before heading out onto the road.

LESSON 5: GEARS

By now you're hopefully able to move away and stop the car, and you've got the hang of steering technique. Now we're onto the gears. In terms of driving, I think this is the best bit: shifting gear! If you're able to practice this lesson, head back to your favourite car park. You're gonna need a straight run, at least the length of a football pitch, to give you room to practice a gear change or two.

Now, in this lesson, I'm going to be talking about:

- Finding your way
- What each gear does and when to change
- How to change gear
- Using the gears on hills
- Changing down to go faster
- The mistakes people make

Let's begin with the position of each gear, and a section we'll call…

Finding Your Way

So far we've met neutral – that we think of as zero gear – and 1st gear, the one we use for moving away and for low-speed manoeuvring.

So, from the driver's seat, with the engine off and the clutch pedal held down, take hold of the gear-stick. Remember that to check the car's in neutral, you either pull the stick gently towards you or push it away. Either way, in neutral, it'll spring back into that central position.

Take a look at the stick. Most have a diagram on the (hilariously named) gear-knob, a map of where each gear's situated. Then feel beneath that to the metal bar connecting the gear-knob to the car itself. It's often buried beneath a cover of soft, plastic fabric that's pretending to be leather! It's usually the length and thickness of a pencil.

Now look back down at the map of the gears. Imagine you're in 4th gear and you want to change into 2nd. To get from 4th, you must move the stick up, into neutral, then follow the line across to the left, then down into 2nd. There are no short cuts. There are no diagonals.

Try it. Be gentle. Move the stick around between gears. Feel the spring. Feel the way you follow the diagram to find each gear. And find reverse. Different cars have different ways of protecting reverse – after all, we don't want you accidentally driving backwards! Some have it all the way over to the right, away from 1st gear. But some have it next to 1st with, perhaps, a lever beneath the gear-knob that you must pull up in order to find reverse.

Feel how 1st and 2nd gears are over to the left, and 5th is over to the right. But also feel how you can't find the middle of the gearbox, how you have to let the spring settle the gear-stick into its neutral position, for both 3rd and 4th. So 3rd is over to the right of 2nd but it's not fully over to the right. No, it's just in the middle. So when you take the gear-stick out of 2nd to change into 3rd, simply relax your grip, and let the stick settle in its neutral position – then gently push it forward into 3rd.

And from 1st gear into 2nd you must hold the stick over to the left. With the stick in 1st, try rolling your hand around the gear-knob so that your palm is facing away from you, towards your Supervisor, then scoop the stick back into 2nd, as if you were scooping nice warm bathwater around yourself. But notice that, if you don't use the scoop technique, how easy it is for the stick to accidentally spring across and fall into 4th gear.

Now, still stationary, change up through the gears, 1st to 5th, without looking down. Picture the position of each gear, picture the map. Remember there are no shortcuts or diagonals – it's all side to side, and forward and back. Feel the movement of the stick. Work against the spring for 1st and 2nd, keeping the stick over to the left. And also for 5th, but this time keeping the stick over to the right. But then, for 3rd and 4th, work with the spring, letting it settle into its neutral position. Gentle movements. Don't force the stick or move it abruptly. Relax with it.

Then go down through the gears. Firstly in sequence: 5th, 4th, 3rd, 2nd, then back into 1st. But then out of sequence, so from 4th, say, back to 2nd.

Now that you've got the feel of the position of each gear, let's talk a little bit about...

What Each Gear Does And When To Change

1st gear you've already met. It's there for moving away and for low speed control. So leaving a parking space or a driveway is done in 1st. Then, as the car speeds up, you change up through the gears in sequence, deciding when to change up based on *the sound of the engine*. We all know that engine noise that kids make, playing with cars! So, as you speed up, you change up, in sequence, based on the sound of the engine.

Around town, in thirty limits, in most cars you really only use 1st, 2nd and 3rd, as 3rd gear and 30mph usually suit each other perfectly. If you want to use 4th around town, be careful, because in 4th most cars want to go faster than thirty, and on your driving test your Examiner will be far more concerned about the speed you're doing than the gear you're using.

Also, a lot of people talk about *getting up into fourth* as soon as possible to save fuel. But the most economical gear for any given situation is the one that you feel gives you the most control. It's all about control. If you're driving well, you're driving economically. And also remember that although many people use 4th in thirty limits they might not actually be driving at thirty! And, as I said, your Examiner's going to be watching your speed like a hawk.

Anyway, cars differ. For all I know you might be learning to drive in an Aston Martin! So, when you start driving on the road, discuss it with your Supervisor and just see which gear feels most comfortable to use when you're at thirty.

Now, let's talk about changing down. Firstly, remember, you generally change up through the gears in sequence. But changing down is done *selectively*.

Selective gear changing means, rather than simply changing down in sequence as you approach, say, a junction, instead you change down directly into the gear you're actually planning on using next. In other words, changing down, we leave gears out.

Changing up selectively is okay – say, 2nd up into 4th – it won't do your car any harm, but it's done far less frequently than when changing down.

So, in everyday driving, you'll be changing down from 4th gear into 2nd, or 3rd into 1st. In fact, if the situation calls for it, you might even find yourself changing down directly from top gear into 1st gear.

Secondly, remember you change up based on the sound of your engine. But you choose which gear to change down into based on miles-per-hour, so based on the actual speed your doing. As a rough guide, round up your speed in miles-per-hour then take away the zero. So, as I've already said, in most cars 30mph suits

3rd gear. Forty suits 4th. Twenty suits 2nd.

Picture yourself approaching a set of traffic lights. You're driving at 40mph in 4th gear. The lights are still some distance away when you see them change from green to red. So you start slowing down…you come off the gas…you start braking…now the clutch is going down…when, happy days, the lights change back to green. Okay, so a quick glance at your speedo and you see that you're now doing around 15mph. So, round that fifteen up to twenty, take away the zero – that gives you a two – so change into 2nd gear and drive away again.

If, in that scenario, you'd either stopped or been virtually stopped, you'd have chosen 1st gear. But if you'd been doing more than twenty, you'd round your speed up to thirty – then take away the zero – and chosen 3rd gear.

Each gear, then, has a range of speeds that it works over. So, using our guide, we said that at, say, 30mph to use 3rd gear. But 3rd gear doesn't only work at thirty. No, its range is from about 15mph below thirty all the way up to 15mph above thirty. So 3rd gear can work from right down at 15mph all the way up to forty-five, with thirty being the middle of 3rd gear's range.

Using this system, 2nd gear works from just above walking pace, up through twenty, all the way up to 35mph. And 4th works from twenty-five up to fifty-five.

So, at 30mph, your car would be happy in any of those three gears – 2nd, 3rd or 4th – but it would be *happiest* in 3rd.

Again, this is only a rough guide, so discuss it with your Supervisor and then, when you're out on the road, again, see how your car feels.

Okay, so now we know the theory of which gear to choose, let's talk about…

How To Change Gear

But just before we do, bear in mind three things. The first is that the single most important thing to remember during a gear change is to keep looking where you're going. Don't look down. Remember you steer with your eyes, not with your hands. So if, during a gear change, you start looking down at the gear-stick, trying to figure-out what to do next, you will likely crash and end up in somebody's front garden!

The second thing is that if you were to time a gear change as if it were an Olympic sport then the stopwatch would start when you press the clutch pedal down, not when you take hold of the gear-stick. Taking hold of the gear-stick is simply preparation for the gear change to come.

So, when changing gear say to yourself: hand down, clutch down. Hand down to the gear-stick in preparation, then clutch down to begin the actual gear change.

Finally, third thing, when the clutch is down for the gear change, make sure your foot lifts off the gas. Generally, if you're changing down this won't be a problem because you'll already be off the gas, slowing the car down. But the changing up sequence now becomes: hand down, clutch down, off the gas. If you don't lift off the gas at this point your engine will get really noisy. It won't do it any harm, but it will scream its head off at you in complaint, and quite possibly, so will your Supervisor!

Anyway, let's work through changing up from 1st gear into 2nd:

- In a straight line, accelerate gently in 1st gear
- Listen to the sound of the engine
- Reach down and find the gear-stick
- Remember, cup your hand, ready to hold the stick over to the left

- Clutch down
- Lift off the gas
- Change gear
- Clutch up gently, over a count of 1...2...3...
- Back on the gas

At the end of the gear change, if you want the car to slow down, leave the gas pedal alone, stay off it. But if you want to continue at the same speed, or to speed up, then you need to get back on the gas. And, ideally, the plan is to get back on the gas as the clutch comes back up. So it's clutch up 1...2...gas back on...3.

Now let's tighten that sequence up:
- Accelerate
- Listen to the engine
- Hand down
- Clutch down
- Off the gas
- Change gear
- Clutch up: 1...2...
- On the gas
- Clutch fully up...3

Finally, then, changing up is:
- Hand down
- Clutch down
- Off the gas
- Change
- Clutch up 1...2...
- On the gas
- Clutch up...3

Remember, changing down is different because you're not generally concerned with the sound of the engine but with the speed of the car. Also, you generally change down because you're slowing down, which means you will be off the gas both before and after the gear change. Easy. So that would be:

- Hand down
- Clutch down
- Change
- Clutch up...1...2...3

Which brings us onto...

Using The Gears On Hills

...and one of the skills that many new drivers find tricky to master: changing down going downhill.

Now, if you think back to when we were discussing the clutch, the problem in changing down going downhill is coasting. Remember that if you press the clutch down going downhill you will speed up unless you brake simultaneously. This means that you'll need to use the brake to control your speed all the way through the gear change.

So, changing down going downhill is:

- Brake gently and stay on the brake
- Hand down
- Stay on the brake!
- Clutch down
- Stay on the brake!
- Change gear
- Stay on the brake!
- Clutch up...1...2...3
- Off the brake

Now, this probably sounds quite straightforward but, as I said, this is a skill that does catch a lot of people out, because if you lift off the brake at any time before the clutch comes back up then you will speed up. And that will come as a shock to both you and your Supervisor if, say, you were changing down in readiness for a tight turn into a side road!

If your car park has a nice downhill section, then practice this skill. But if it doesn't, this is something that you must practice in a straight line first. Don't wait until you're actually approaching a downhill junction before trying it for the first time!

Now for some good news. Changing down going uphill is much easier because your car will be naturally slowing down throughout the gear change. Much less drama!

That's changing down. Changing *up* going downhill is also easy because as you press the clutch down to start the gear change your car will continue to speed up as it coasts down the hill. In fact, on a steep downhill you don't really need to use the engine in between gears at all. The gradient will effectively do the accelerating for you.

Changing up going uphill is trickier though. Again, it's down to coasting and the effect the gradient has on the car. So changing up uphill you need to drive a little faster, say 10mph faster, than on a level road for each gear change. This extra speed's necessary to carry you through the gear change while the hill's trying to slow you down.

Hills, and especially uphill, also has an effect in our next subject...

Changing Down To Go Faster

Imagine you're going away for a well-earned break, a long weekend. You're gonna need to pack, so from the bottom of your wardrobe you drag out your five bags. You have a small ruck-sack, handy for an overnight, and a big suitcase that you nor-mally use for longer holidays. Then there are three other bags, each of which fits somewhere in between those other two. So, which one should you take? Do you want to travel light or go large, or somewhere in between?

Now, your car's engine thinks about its gears in the same way as you're thinking about those bags. The biggest one is great be-cause you can carry the most stuff, but it's heavy. That's like 5th gear. Your engine can pack lots of *Miles per Hour* but it finds it heavy to carry. The overnight bag, then, is like 1st gear. Great for nipping about, easy to carry, for sure, but it can't pack many MPH.

Now imagine you're arriving at your budget hotel. The lift's broken. Your room's on the fourth floor. And, oh dear, you've brought your biggest bag, the one your engine calls 5th gear. Well, by the time you're halfway up the first flight of stairs you're already wishing that you could swap it for a smaller bag.

But when you're *driving* up a steep hill, rather than walking up steep stairs, you can swap. You can change gear. So, rather than having your engine struggling to carry 5th all the way to the top of the hill, you can change down into a lower gear to give your engine a lighter load to carry. You're changing down to go faster.

So, obviously, 3rd gear, or whatever gear you change down into, can't carry as many miles-per-hour as 4th or 5th, but sometimes, as I've said, if your engine's struggling, give it a smaller load to carry, to help it climb that hill. Or to help it accelerate...

Imagine, then, catching up with a slow-moving vehicle, a tractor, say, that's doing 25mph while you're in 4th gear. As you now know, your car will just about drive along in 4th at twenty-five. But it won't effectively accelerate, because 4th is just too heavy a load for your engine to carry at such a low speed. So, to overtake the tractor, rather than lugging along in 4th, change down into 3rd – to give your engine a lighter load – so that it can then accelerate much more quickly.

Which brings us on to the final part of this lesson, the...

Mistakes People Make

The main mistake involves sequence. Remember, it's *hand down, clutch down.* So you reach down for the gear-stick, think about what you're going to do, then clutch down. When the clutch goes down, that's the start of the gear change. Reaching down first, to take hold of the gear-stick, is just preparation for the gear change to come.

So the mistake people make is pressing the clutch pedal down first, then hunting around for the gear-stick, then changing gear. This makes the actual gear change take much longer than necessary because you're starting the gear change before you've even found the gear-stick!

But the other problem with falling into the habit of *clutch down, hand down* is that almost everyone who does it eventually ends up looking down at the gear-stick during the gear change. It's like night follows day. Clutch down – look at the gear-stick – hand down! And looking down at the gear-stick as you change gear just isn't acceptable on test. Your Examiner will mark you down. You're expected to look where you're going, not at what you're doing.

The other mistake that happens on test is that Examiners don't like to see you changing gear while you're turning the steering wheel. The steering has priority. Steer first, then change gear. And that includes when you're, say, pulling out of a side road and the engine's starting to get a bit noisy as you accelerate. Don't worry about it. A bit of noise for a couple of seconds won't do any harm, even if you can almost feel your Supervisor willing you to change up!

However, it's okay to change gear when you have the steering-wheel turned, say, halfway round a roundabout, but you're just holding it still, not actually turning it. So it's when you're turning the wheel that the gear change is going to have to wait for a few more seconds.

So it should be steer then gear. Which is something else to practice before changing up to Lesson 6, where we'll discuss the clutch, and the four essential clutch-control skills that, between them, will give you complete low-speed control of your car.

LESSON 6: CLUTCH CONTROL AND MOVING AWAY ON HILLS

If you're going to be able to practice this lesson, you'll need a car park or very quiet road, but one with a nice gentle hill. Nothing too steep, but steep enough that you can tell that your car will definitely roll when you release the brakes.

Now, if you've followed the lessons through to this point, hopefully you're starting to get a feel for using the clutch and you now realise how important it is in helping you to control the car. In this lesson, I'm going to be taking your skills up to the next level, so this is going to be a busy lesson! I'll be looking at:

- Controlled coasting downhill
- Moving away downhill
- Controlled coasting using momentum
- Holding point control
- The dreaded hill-start
- The angled start

Coasting, as you now know, is what happens to a moving car when the clutch is pressed down, the way it rolls along, like a freewheeling bicycle. So, unlike a car's other controls, the clutch doesn't have a direct effect on the car – it doesn't actually make it slow down or speed up, it simply lets it roll. So when you're coasting, it's the gradient that's really in control of the car – uphill you'll stop, downhill you'll speed up. So…

Controlled Coasting Downhill

…is essentially understanding the effect a hill will have on the speed of your car and being able to work with it. In other words, at really low speed, using downhill gradients as a kind of engine, and uphill gradients as a kind of brake.

Picture yourself in busy traffic, facing downhill. The car ahead of you moves forward two-or-three car lengths then stops again. So, to move up safely behind him, with your clutch in and in 1st gear you press the footbrake – not the gas – and release the handbrake. Then to move, you keep the clutch down but gently ease up a little on the footbrake until your car starts to move. Your car's rolling. It's coasting. But you're *controllin' the rollin'* with the footbrake! This is *controlled coasting*.

But don't take your foot off the brake completely because then you will roll away, faster and faster, like a rollercoaster. The hill will be in control, not you.

To practice, facing downhill, have the clutch in, in 1st gear, with the footbrake on and the handbrake off. Then, keeping the clutch firmly down the entire time, ease gently off the footbrake – but, as I said, not completely off the footbrake – stay with it, stay in control of the hill. Use the footbrake gently. Let the car roll a few metres then stop. Stay on the brake. Stay in control. Remember, downhill controlled coasting is controllin' the rollin'. So…

Moving Away Downhill

…is easy because your car will simply start to roll forward the moment you release the brakes. In fact, on a steep downhill, you might not even need 1st gear, you might prefer to use 2nd. After all, 1st gear's really only to get a stationary car moving, so if the hill's going to do it for you, you don't need 1st.

And you don't need to set the gas either. Again, if the car's going to roll away for you, you don't need to bring the engine into play until the car's moving.

So, moving away downhill goes like this:
- Clutch down
- 1st or 2nd gear
- Footbrake on
- Handbrake off...
- Then, release the footbrake
- Clutch up...1...2...3

Okay, so that's using a downhill gradient to our advantage. Now let's talk about...

Controlled Coasting Using Momentum

Picture yourself approaching a roundabout on a level road. So there's no downhill here to keep you moving. You look to your right and see one car coming around the roundabout towards you, so you slow down and drop down into 2nd gear. The plan is to allow that car to pass then join the roundabout immediately behind it. But, turns out, that car's going slower than you had realised, so you're going to have to slow down even more, down to below 10mph.

Now, most cars won't go below 10mph in 2nd gear with the clutch up without complaining. The car will shudder and possibly even stall if you try to go any slower with the clutch up. So, as your speed drops down to below ten, you need to press the clutch down. And now you've got two options:
- Change down into 1st gear, join the roundabout, then

immediately change back up into 2nd
- Stay in 2nd and use the momentum of your moving car to use controlled coasting

The first of these two options will be difficult to do smoothly. You'll almost certainly end up with a shuddering clutch and a noisy engine. So, let's try option two, then! It takes a bit of practice, but this technique allows you to stay in 2nd gear, but to drive away again smoothly, even though your speed's dropped down to below 10mph.

To practice controlled coasting using momentum, try this:
- Find a level piece of road
- Drive in 2nd gear at, say, 20mph
- Come off the gas and allow the speed to drop down to 10mph
- Clutch down and let the speed drop to, say, 5mph
- Give the engine a little gas
- Ease the clutch up very gently, feeling the engine pulling you again
- But don't lift the clutch off completely until your speed's back up to 10mph

Essentially, as long as the road's either downhill or level, provided your car's still moving you'll not need to change back down into 1st gear. You can just stay in 2nd and get moving again quickly and smoothly, even if your speed's down to below 10mph.

So 1st gear is for when you're stationary or virtually stationary, especially when you're going uphill. Otherwise, as I said, 2nd gear will often be smoother. This is a technique you'll be using all the time. You'll be using it when emerging from those junctions where the view of the main road is quite good and the road ahead seems to be clear as you approach it. It means you'll be going slowly enough to stop easily if you need to, but quick enough to slip away in 2nd gear if the road turns out to be clear.

Now let's move on to uphill control. And let's begin by picturing a little boy out playing with his football on a hilly street. He wants to kick the ball up the hill to his friend. So he places it down then takes a few steps back to take his run-up. Except, his ball doesn't stay still. No, it rolls down the street after him. To stop the ball from rolling down the hill, then, the boy will either need to hold the ball still, like a brake, or use power to kick the ball up the hill.

Now, your car works like that football. It naturally wants to roll downhill. So to stop it rolling away you're going to need either a brake or engine power, and you're going to need to practice a skill called...

Holding Point Control

I've previously described – in fact, I'm sure you're sick of hearing it – the clutch as working like a tap, controlling the flow of power from the engine to the wheels in the same way as a tap controls the flow of water. So when the clutch pedal is held down the tap is off. No power flows.

Now the biting point, as you know, is the point where the clutch pedal has come up far enough to allow power to drip through to the wheels. We call that Clutch 1. But the *holding point* is where the clutch is a fraction higher – at Clutch 2 – where the power's trickling through to the wheels.

So, on a level road, at Clutch 2, your car starts moving, but on a steep uphill it doesn't. On a steep uphill it holds still.

To find the holding point, put your car in 1st gear, handbrake on, and ease the clutch up gently, above the biting point, to the point where the bonnet lifts up, just a centimetre-or-two. Then keep it there for a couple of seconds before pressing the clutch back down again.

That point, where the bonnet's up a couple of centimetres, is the point where the car will hold still if it's facing uphill and you release the handbrake. It won't roll back. But it won't lurch forward either. At the holding point, even without brakes, the car just holds still.

To practice, have the car facing uphill, in 1st gear, handbrake on. Then, with a little gas, use the clutch to lift the bonnet up those couple of centimetres and release the handbrake...

Okay, so what did your car do?

- If it rolled back, either the clutch wasn't quite high enough to begin with or else you pressed it back down as you released the handbrake
- If it lurched forward, the clutch was up too high
- But if it stayed still...well done. A round of applause!

To practice further, try this. So, facing uphill, 1st gear, handbrake on. Then find the holding point and release the handbrake. Now, this time, with the car holding still, press the clutch down a few centimetres to deliberately let the car roll back a couple of metres...but then try to ease the clutch gently back up again to catch yourself as you roll. You'll need to be really smooth with the clutch.

As you practice this, ask your Supervisor to keep an eye out for you, to make sure there's nothing behind you. And if, at any time, you find yourself panicking, simply press the clutch down and use the footbrake to stop the car.

As you get the hang of this you can play with the holding point, and you can play with the clutch... Squeeze it down to roll back. Ease it up to stop again. Clutch a bit higher to creep forward, then squeeze it back down to find the holding point again.

Your goal here is to be able to make the car do what you want without using the brakes. Hold still, roll back, creep forward. Now, this is an essential skill but it takes a lot of practice, and you might not necessarily get the hang of it first time out. The good news, though, is that once you have it, this fine control of the clutch – this clutch *finesse*, as the Americans would say – stays with you for life.

But a word of warning. Back in Lesson 3, I mentioned that the clutch mechanism, so the bit down in the engine that your clutch pedal controls, works using a friction plate. And things that use friction, including your very expensive clutch, can wear out. Now, practising, as we've described here, will do your clutch no harm at all, provided you remember two things:

- **To practice for no more than 30 seconds at a time**
- **To keep your engine speed no higher than 2,000 RPM**

Now, on test, one of the things you'll be asked to do is…

The Dreaded Hill Start

So, your Examiner wants you to move away uphill, without stalling or rolling back. To do this, to prevent the engine stalling, you're going to need some gas. Trying to move away uphill on tick-over just won't work. And to prevent the car from rolling back, you're going to need to use the holding point.

So, the hill-start procedure is:

- Clutch in
- 1st gear
- Set the gas
- Clutch 1: the bite…
- Then, up a bit higher – to Clutch 2 – the holding point
- Keep your feet still
- Mirror
- Signal

- Blind spot
- Door mirror…
- Then, release the handbrake
- Clutch 3: so all the way up, but lifting it gently
- A little more gas than usual to drive away

The final skill we're going to discuss in this lesson is, again, something you'll be asked to do on test. It's called…

The Angled Start

What happens is this, your Examiner asks you to, 'Pull over on the left-hand-side of the road close to a parked car.'

Close here means stopping so that you can just see the road surface between you and the other car.

Then, when you're asked to move away again, you'll need to keep control of the clutch, to keep your car moving slowly, as you steer out quickly to get around the other car, then straighten up again, all under control.

The other thing to remember here is that, as well as traffic coming up behind you, you'll also need to watch out for traffic approaching you from the front. This is because that whenever you're moving away from a parked position you must give way to any moving traffic. Now, usually, as you know, that means cars coming up behind you, but here, because you're moving out from behind a parked car, and so because you're going to have to move out onto the wrong side of the road, you must also give way to traffic coming towards you.

So this manoeuvre needs good coordination and good clutch control. It also needs nerves of steel on the part of your Supervisor! So it wouldn't be a good idea to practice it until both of you are sure that your control is up to it.

LESSON 7: ANCILLARY CONTROLS, SAFETY CHECKS & THEORY TEST

After all your hard work back in Lesson 6, you get an easier time of it here, so, even though this lesson has quite a daunting title, we're just going to be covering your car's ancillary controls – so the lights, wipers, etc – and also a few simple safety checks that you can do from inside the car. We'll also take the opportunity to talk about the Theory Test, and also to put some of that theory into practice, with The Real Life Hazard Perception Challenge! Bet you can't wait!

So, to re-cap, in this lesson it's:

- Ancillary Controls
- Safety Checks
- Theory Test Questions
- Theory Test Hazard Perception
- The Real Life Hazard Perception Challenge!

Let's get started. The...

Ancillary Controls

...are the controls that you'll be using every day, but not the ones that you need to make the car move. On test you'll be expected to know how these work, so if it rains you'll be expected to know how to use the wipers! And you'll also be asked to demonstrate to your Examiner at least one of these controls as part of your test.

Now, all cars are different, so here you'll be getting your Supervisor to run through how these things work specifically in your car. Then, to practice with these new controls, once you've worked out how everything works and what everything does, try using these controls while driving around your favourite car park. You don't want to be panicking, trying to figure out how, say, the wipers work, in the middle of rush-hour traffic!

So here we're going to take a quick look at the:

- Lights & Horn
- Washers and Wipers
- Heater and Air Conditioning
- Warning Lights

So, where's the hooter – the horn – on your car? Go on then…you know you want to! *Beep beep*!

Next…let there be light! The first position on the light switch, your sidelights, puts on your tail lights and your low-powered front lights. The sidelights are also known as the *parking lights* because these are really just for when you're stationary, so, for example, parked on an unlit country road, or pulled over on a city street.

The second position on your light switch is for your dipped headlights. You'll probably see a green light come on, on the dashboard. *Dipped* means they're focussed down and to the left, so as not to dazzle oncoming drivers, to not temporarily blind them.

Use your dipped beam when you're driving, not just sidelights.

Remember, sidelights are just parking lights. So use dipped headlights when you're driving at night or in poor visibility. Poor visibility means, even though you can see just fine, it may be harder than usual for other drivers to see you. So in heavy rain, say, or at dusk, use dipped headlights.

But don't leave your dipped headlights on when your engine's switched off. In time, you'll flatten the battery and so your engine might not start. Also, switch off your headlights if you're parking over on the wrong side of the road, because as the dip on the headlights is to the left, your headlights will shine directly into the eyes of oncoming drivers, dazzling them.

The next stage on your car's lights is full beam, also known as main beam. Full beam is brighter than dipped, and the focus of the light is thrown further forward and straight ahead, rather than just down and to the left. When your lights are on full beam you get a blue warning light.

Only use full beam on unlit roads when it won't dazzle anyone. So if there's anyone ahead of you, either travelling towards you or in the same direction as you, or even waiting to emerge from a side road, then just use dipped beam.

You can only switch to full beam if your dipped headlights are already on, but, even if your headlights are off, you can still flash the headlights – that's a quick burst of full beam. This is generally done by pulling the indicator switch back towards you.

Now, officially – so that means, according to the *Highway Code* – the headlight flasher's only function is to warn other drivers that you're there. So it's a visible, rather than audible, version of your horn.

But be wary of cars flashing their lights at you, and don't take it for granted that you know what the flash means. Communication breakdowns happen because different drivers use their headlight flasher to mean different things. Some are telling you to get out of their way, some are telling you that they're going to let you go ahead of them, some are warning you of a hazard ahead, while others are just saying hello!

Now, on your driving test, if you're absolutely certain that another driver's headlight flash is meant for you, and you're absolutely certain what that other driver means by it, then you can act on it, you don't have to just sit there. But you must be *absolutely* certain. However, on test, you're absolutely not allowed to flash your lights at anyone else – unless, that is, you're using the *Highway Code*'s definition of what the headlight flasher's for, so you're warning someone that you're there.

Your car will also have fog lights – either one or two at the back, and possibly two at the front. And, on your dash, you'll have warning lights to let you know when the fog lights are on.

So, when should you use your fog lights? Er...when it's foggy! Well, the *Highway Code* says when visibility is down to 100 metres. But, seriously, what does 100 metre visibility really look like? I have no idea. So, when it's foggy – although not the official wording – kind of makes sense.

Anyway, the front fog lights are not to make your car look like a rally car, and the rear ones are not to make your car more visible in the rain. Essentially, they're for when it's foggy.

Using your front fog lights when it isn't foggy will dazzle other drivers because the light is bright but not focused down and to the left. So, unlike your dipped headlights, front fog lights are just bright splashes of light.

Now, some guys like using their front fog lights instead of dipped headlights. It's a cosmetic thing, so giving their car some rally style. The problem with this, though, is that not only is it illegal because the front fogs will, as I said, dazzle other drivers, but also because their light pattern is focused close to the car, seriously limiting how far ahead you can see.

And using your rear fog lights when it isn't foggy can also be dangerous. The traffic following you might not be able to see your brake lights clearly because of the brightness of your fog lights, especially if the design of your tail lights places your brake lights and fog lights close together. And again, same as the front, it's illegal to use rear fog lights unless it's foggy – so, visibility down to less than 100 metres.

Next, the washers and wipers. For the wipers to work with your engine switched off, you'll need the car's electrics to be switched on. This is sometimes known as *ignition*. It's when the key is turned part way, far enough round to power-up the dashboard warning lights. On a key-card system, you might need to put the key in the *reader.*

For your windscreen wipers, the first click on the switch will either be for an automatic system, which senses when rain's falling on your windscreen, or *intermittent* – when the wipers swish every few seconds. The second click of the switch has the wipers wiping steadily across the windscreen. And the third click has your car thinking it's a lifeboat, the wipers now going top speed!

To wash the screen, generally you pull the wiper switch back towards you and hold it for a few seconds. This will fire a jet of water at the windscreen, while the wipers swish backwards and forwards. This is something you might be asked to do on your driving test.

Finally, there's the rear-window washer and wiper. On some cars, if you have the wipers on, the rear wiper will come on automatically when you go into reverse gear.

Okay, so now let's move onto the heating system, because the other occasion when you'll find yourself needing to clear your windows is when they steam-up, which often happens on rainy days.

Now, if at all possible, avoid wiping steamed-up windows with your bare hands. Yes, smearing the condensation around may give you a temporary improvement, but it will only be temporary, and it'll soon dry to a smudgy mess. It's far better to use your *demisters* instead.

Get your Supervisor to explain the workings of your car's heater and demisters. The demisters work by blasting warm air up onto the windscreen, rather than down onto your feet. Using this in conjunction with your heated rear window and, if your car has one, the electrically heated windscreen, will soon sort things out.

Now, when you first start the engine, an array of coloured warning lights illuminates the dashboard for a couple of seconds before they – hopefully – go out. Hopefully because if one of the warning lights stays on, or comes on when you're driving, it spells trouble. Just how much trouble is defined by the colour. An amber light is bad, a red light is really bad!

Switch your electrics on and off a few times to give you chance to take a look at these warning lights. On test you might be asked to check a particular system by switching the electrics on and simply confirming that the warning light has gone off. Pretty simple. But only if you know where the warning lights are. There are also a couple of other...

Safety Checks

...that you can do from the comfort of the driver's seat that, again, you might be asked about on your driving test.

You can check the basic function of the brakes by simply pressing down on the brake pedal and pulling up on the handbrake lever. You should feel resistance from both. So if the footbrake flops to the floor, or your handbrake lever comes up to your armpit, you have a problem.

Your car's powered steering is powered by the engine. So, when the engine's running, the steering-wheel should turn easily. If it doesn't, if it feels the same as it does when the engine's switched off, then the powered steering's not working.

So that's a run-down of some of the *safety questions*, the questions you'll be asked on your practical test. But you've got a whole bunch more questions to answer before you can even apply for a practical test, because first, you've got to pass your...

Theory Test

The theory test has two parts, the written questions and the *hazard perception* video test, and you must pass both parts at the same time for an overall test pass. So you can't just pass the written questions one week then go back in a couple of weeks' time to do the hazard perception part.

When you arrive at your local theory test centre, your provisional licence is checked and you're asked to put anything you have with you – bags, mobile phone, whatever – into a locker. And *you* might also be checked! It's not unusual to be asked to pull up your sleeves so that the test centre staff can check that you haven't written anything on your arms!

Anyway, if you do manage to make it past security, you head over to your allotted computer terminal and start with the question part of the test. This is done as fifty multiple-choice questions. You are given loads of time for this part of the test – you could do a hundred questions, let alone fifty, in the time available, so don't rush. Take your time.

Various languages are available as well as readers to help you along, if necessary. But if you would like to avail yourself of one of these services, you should book it in advance. Otherwise, it's just assumed that you'll take the test in English, and read the questions yourself.

If you get stuck on a question, or you've answered it but would like a chance to look over it again, then you can flag individual questions and come back to them again at the end. However, I think your best bet, based on anecdotal evidence from many hundreds of past pupils, is to make your way through the questions, one at a time, answering them all – even if your answer is just an educated guess – and to leave the flag option well alone. Many people go back to flagged questions, doubting themselves, then change what turns out to be the correct answer to a wrong answer. Happens all the time.

Preparing for your theory is best done using one of the Apps available. A good one will be kept up to date with all the latest questions, will allow you to focus on particular topics, and will keep a record of your practice test scores. So there's no need anymore to load your desk with more books than a philosophy student, it's all on your phone.

However, there's one book still well worth a careful read: The *Highway Code*. The *Highway Code* gives you the rules of the road. Sounds boring, perhaps, but you wouldn't try your hand at a new sport without knowing the rules, would you? And investing in a paper copy allows you to make notes in the margins and underline stuff. Proper old school but it still works!

It covers pretty much everything you'll need for your theory test and it does it in a short, sharp format. The problem with the Apps is that they essentially just ask questions then tell you whether you were right or wrong, whereas the *Highway Code* gives you the information up front.

For example, did you know that there's a colour system of reflectors and cat's eyes used to help you work out what lane you're in at night or in fog? There are at least a dozen questions based on this system that you could be asked in your theory test, but, in just one paragraph, the *Highway Code* gives you all the information you'll need to answer those questions.

However, if you don't even know about the system, let alone how it works, then what's the point of trying to answer questions about it on your App? All that will do is highlight what you *don't* know. So read through the *Highway Code*, along with using a theory App.

Incidentally, one way to remember how the colour system works goes like this: picture an RAC van – one of those orange, recovery service vehicles – sitting, first in the queue, at a red traffic light. Got that? An RAC van at a red light. Now, RAC: **R**ed, **A**mber, **C**entre of the road. So the red cat's eyes are on the left-hand-side of, say, a motorway, amber on the right, and then you have the centre – on a motorway that's the grassy *central reservation*.

Next, think of the traffic light that the van's waiting at. Traffic lights have red, amber and green lights. Red and amber have already been used in our RAC, so that leaves green. Green, then, is the odd one out. So green is just used for slip lanes, side roads and lay-bys.

Finally, our van's first in the queue at the lights, so it's waiting on the white line. White cat's eyes go along the white lane-lines.

So, a question might be: *you're driving along on a three-lane motorway at night. There are white reflectors to your left and right. What lane are you in?*

Well, as we've seen, the system on a three-lane motorway would be red to the left, amber to the right, and white along the lane lines. So it'd be: red, white, white, amber. The answer, then, would be the middle lane, lane two.

Anyway, the point is, the *Highway Code* gives you the chance to work these things out for yourself, rather than just bombarding you with questions.

Now, once you've finished the fifty questions, it's on to the Hazard Perception part of the test. This is done in fourteen one-minute video clips during which you're on the hunt for fifteen hazards. Yep, you've got it – one of the clips has two hazards.

Once you begin the hazard perception test you can't pause it. The clips just keep on comin'! So it's finger on the buzzer... Oh, but you don't have to point a cursor at the hazards. You simply click the button.

The main problem people seem to have with this test is in understanding what it's actually about. Firstly, the clue's in the name: *hazard perception*. *Hazard* here is essentially defined as something that makes you slow down or stop. And *perception* means to be observant and aware. So this test is not just hazard identification. It's not about waiting until an obvious hazard fills the screen. It's about watching for clues.

The second thing that catches people out is thinking that they're only allowed to press the button once per clip. That's not the case. You might, on certain clips, press the button three-or-four times. So if you were to press the button after spotting something – say, a car approaching the end of a side road – thinking it might pull-out, you're not penalised if it turns out that the car just stops, where it's supposed to, without any drama. No. You saw the clue. You pressed the button. It's fine. If it turns out to be a false alarm, that's not a problem.

Having said that, if you press the button a couple of times in quick succession, like you're playing some sort of rogue special-forces video-game, then you'll be told by the computer that you're cheating and you won't score any points for that clip.

The final problem with this test is with what we'll call the *scoring window*. So, picture the scene unfolding on the computer screen before you. You're driving along a virtual country road, approaching a bend. Then, just before the bend you spot a triangular warning sign – miles away, barely visible without binoculars. It's the one with a cow in the middle of it. A-ha, you think, a potential hazard, cows crossing just around this next bend. So you press the button. And, right enough, your car carries on around the bend…and there's the hazard, an old farmer coaxing a herd of cows across the road. Well done, you!

Except that, at the end of the test, you discover that you scored zero points on that particular clip, because you apparently pressed the button too early! Now, I realise this doesn't sound fair, but it is possible to be too clever. So the trick is to spot the clue and press the button, but then to count to yourself a steady…1…2…3…and press the button again, just to be on the safe side.

So, the scoring window, for our imagined clip with the cows, starts just before the sign, not miles before it. So if you press the button just before the sign, you score the full five points. And then, from the start of the scoring window, up to the point where you actually see the cows crossing the road, the score counts down, like a rocket about to blast off…5…4…3…2…1!

So, practice hazard perception clips on your theory test App.

But you can also play…

The Real Life Hazard Perception Challenge!

Okay, so the way this works: as you're being driven somewhere, try literally commentating on what's going on, out there. Say it out loud. And try to keep talking. So look well ahead, right up the road, see what's happening. Give yourself plenty to talk about.

Sounds easy, doesn't it? But this is something you'd be asked to do if you ever took an advanced driving test. It gets you thinking, really thinking.

So, warn yourself of the kids messing about at the bus stop, mention the car leaving the petrol station, and congratulate yourself on catching a glimpse of the reflection of that bike behind the van. Try actually saying what the road signs mean. Say where you think the cars on a roundabout are going to go.

Then try pointing-out to yourself ten potential dangers in one minute. Try The Real Life Hazard Perception Challenge!

Then get whoever's driving you about to try it. Eh...they're not smiling now, are they?!

LESSON 8: MIRROR, SIGNAL, MANOEUVRE

Okay, so in your *Highway Code* you'll see the initials MSM used. It stands for: Mirror Signal Manoeuvre Let's get straight to it and start with the...

Mirrors

Mirror, signal, manoeuvre...it's the driving instructor's mantra. We say it all the time because it's the system your Examiner will expect you to use on your driving test. Your name might be Lewis Hamilton, but if you don't use the mirror, signal, manoeuvre routine, you don't pass!

By the way, when I say *manoeuvre* in this context, I'm talking about a situation where you'll need to change your speed or change your course. And change your *course* essentially means steering, so for a junction or a lane change or a parked car.

So, on your test, whatever situation you find yourself having to deal with, you must start by looking in your mirror. The system is mirror *then* signal *then* manoeuvre.

Mirror first. Then one of the three S's. So it's mirror before you:

- **S**ignal
- **S**teer
- Or change your **S**peed

So, if your Examiner says, 'At the end of the road, turn left', he expects you to look in your mirror before you either signal or start slowing down for the junction. And when he sees a parked car up ahead, he will watch closely to see that you check your mirror before you move out to pass that car. And if he sees a green light up ahead, he will watch both you and the lights to see that – if the lights change – you use your mirror before you brake.

Mirrors, then, are a big deal on your test. Failing to use them correctly is one of the main reasons for…er…failing.

Ah, yes, and remember your car has *mirrors* – plural, more than one. Remember, as well as your rear-view mirror you also have door mirrors. And then there are your *blind spots* to consider as well – those areas just over your shoulders that the door mirrors don't quite cover.

A blind-spot check on the move is just a quick glance over either your left or right shoulder, depending on the way you're going. Literally one-or-two seconds. That's it. It would be far too dangerous to spend any longer than that looking behind you, rather than where you're going. And remember, the blind spot is right there, just over your shoulder. Don't try to spin round in your seat, or look back along the road behind you – you have mirrors for that!

Okay, so all of these – the rear-view mirror, the door mirrors and the blind-spot checks – must be part of your mirror, signal, manoeuvre routine.

So, if you're, changing lanes from left to right, it'd be:
- Rear-view mirror
- Right door-mirror
- Indicate right
- Right blind-spot glance
- All clear?
- Change lanes

When changing lanes, if it's busy, you might have to check your door mirror several times, looking for a gap to move into. And if a big vehicle's passing you, glance into the blind-spot as it passes, in case another – smaller – vehicle is following closely behind it.

Okay. What else? Approaching a red traffic light, when you're turning left, would be something like:

- Rear-view mirror
- Indicate left
- Brake and stop
- Then, when the lights change…
- Look for cyclists in your left door-mirror
- Left blind spot glance
- Turn left

And finally, turning right into a side road:

- Rear-view mirror
- Right door-mirror
- Indicate right
- If possible, position over to the right
- Another door-mirror check, looking for, say, overtaking motorbikes
- Turn right

So that's the system used by your Examiner to mark your use of the mirrors on test.

But there's more…

If it was only necessary to use your mirrors before you signalled, or whatever, then it could theoretically be possible to drive for an hour up a motorway and not bother with your mirrors at all.

But the key to using your mirrors correctly is to always know what's going on around you – so *at all times* as an Examiner might say – and not just for the couple of seconds before you make a particular manoeuvre.

The *Highway Code* suggests using your mirrors *frequently*. This is good advice. During your first few lessons, if you drove in heavy traffic, your Supervisor could happily take the mirrors off the car and you wouldn't even notice. You'd be too busy watching where you're going to worry about anything else.

But an experienced driver, in that same heavy traffic, would be a nervous wreck unless his mirrors were adjusted perfectly, just how he likes them. The experienced driver, then, likes to be aware of the *big picture*.

Picture yourself driving into work on a fairly busy road – two lanes going in the same direction, driving along at 30mph – when, suddenly, the car ahead of you hits the brakes and stops.

Now, if you're aware of the big picture, so if you're aware of, say, the van in the lane alongside you, you will brake hard and stay in a straight line. You will instinctively know not to swerve into the other lane. But if you haven't been using your mirrors, and so you haven't seen the van, you might assume that the lane alongside you is clear. You might swerve.

So if you're suddenly forced into action and you *then* look in your mirrors it's already too late. You're like the ostrich with its head in the sand: you can't see a problem so you assume there isn't one. But if you use your mirrors constantly, keeping yourself updated on the traffic behind and alongside you, you will always be aware of the big picture.

Okay, so you know what's going on around you. Now, how are you going to let other people know what you're going to do next? How are you going to communicate?

Well, indicators are the main way a driver communicates with other people, the main way he…

Signals

...what he's planning on doing next. So an indicator is just one type of signal – a flashing orange light. But a signal can be as subtle as a nod of the head. Your brake lights, then, are a signal. Your reversing light is a signal. And your position in the road is a signal.

If you're positioned properly, waiting to make a right turn, but you're indicating left, other drivers will still know you're turning right. They'll just assume you've got the wrong indicator on. Your position in the road signals where you're going, more so than your indicator does.

That's one of the things that can be confusing for us when we see a lorry turning. A lorry driver will often position his vehicle differently from the cars around him. He might need to swing out to take a wide turn at a roundabout or a side road, sometimes even using the wrong side of the road.

And talking of confusing... *Not* indicating is just as much a signal as *actually* indicating. I mean, how many junctions do you pass on your morning commute? How many junctions where you signal that you're continuing along the main road by not indicating?

That's the reason people get so annoyed by drivers who don't indicate at junctions. Because, by not indicating, they're actively telling other people that they're not turning. So by not indicating they're effectively signalling that they're going straight on.

But if an indicator is a signal to others, and if there's definitely nobody else about, then surely there's no need to indicate? It'd be like waving goodbye to a friend after they've already closed the door! Completely pointless.

But, on a driving test, there is a strong argument for indicating anyway, even if there's clearly nobody else around, just in case. After all, your Examiner won't fault you for indicating at a junction even if there's nobody else about. I mean, where's the harm? But he will fault you if you choose not to indicate but then somebody catches you out by turning up unexpectedly.

So, it's up to you. If you're moving away, pulling over, or dealing with a junction, and you're absolutely certain that nobody will benefit from you using an indicator, then it's okay to choose not to. But in town, often people will benefit from your indicator even if you're in a lane that's only for traffic going in one particular direction.

Say you're approaching a set of traffic lights, a set where there's a lane marked with a nice big arrow – a lane that's just for turning left. So you might think there's not much point indicating. I mean, if you're in that lane, surely everyone knows you're turning left?

Well, not necessarily. All the local drivers will know, but what about strangers just passing through? Or, if you're stationary, waiting for the lights to change, maybe your car's the one covering the arrow, hiding it from other drivers. And what about those pedestrians, standing there, waiting for the green man to come on? Do they all know the lane you're in is left-turn-only? Who knows? So stick one on, just in case.

When using your indicators, timing when to put them on – and switch them off again, for that matter – is an important factor. Say you're moving away from the side of the road, or changing lanes on a busy dual-carriageway, it's important that you don't shock other drivers by sticking on your indicator just as they're about to pass you. They'll think you haven't seen them, that you're going to pull out. You'll scare the life out of them!

Sometimes you'll need to turn your indicators off to *break a signal*. That's when you, say, change lanes in order to turn at a junction that's still a good distance away. So, you indicate once for the lane change – then break the signal for a few seconds – then indicate again as you get closer to the junction. That way, following traffic doesn't think you've changed lanes then just accidentally kept your indicator on. They see two distinct signals: one for the lane change, one for the junction.

And at a junction, when you're coming up to the end of a road, the driver following you knows that you've got to slow down, and he knows that you've got to turn one way or the other, so there's no need for you to indicate miles away. A few car lengths from the junction will do. But, on the other hand, if you're approaching your turn-off on a fast main road, it's good to get your indicator on nice-n-early, early enough to warn following traffic that you're about to slow down ready to make a turn.

So, indicator timing is a balancing act. You want to make sure people know what you're planning on doing in good time, but you're also trying not to indicate so early that you might mislead them.

On test, if you're asked to take the next road on the left, but there's a petrol station between you and that road, wait until you've passed the petrol station before indicating left for the turn. And if you're asked to take the next road on the left, but there's a car parked just before the turn, then wait until you're out, positioned to pass the parked car, before indicating left. Don't indicate left then move out to the right.

After a junction, generally the indicators will turn themselves off. You might remember, from Lesson 2, that this is called *self cancelling*. So as you straighten up it isn't usually necessary to switch them off. But sometimes it is. Sometimes they don't go off, especially after moving away or changing lanes. Then it's important for you to realise your indicator's still on, and to turn it off. They're really misleading if you leave them on, and the last thing you want on test is for your Examiner to have to tell you to turn an indicator off. Oh, and click your indicators on and off nice-n-gently with your fingertips. Try to avoid letting go of the steering-wheel to do it. There's no need and, again, you could be marked-down on test.

Another point, regarding the test, is that you should only give signals that tell other people what you're going to do. Don't give any signals to tell other people what you'd like them to do. So, no waving other traffic past, when you're in the middle of a parking manoeuvre. If they decide to pass, that's up to them, not up to you.

And that includes using your headlight flasher or your car's horn. As I said in Lesson 7, they're just there to warn other people of your presence, if you think they haven't seen you yet. They're not there for you to use to tell them to go, or to wait, or whatever.

But, having said that, if somebody else signals to you in some way – say they wave to let you out of a side road – it's fine for you to go, provided, again, as I said in Lesson 7, that you're sure that it is you they're signalling to, and that you're sure you know what it is they mean. So if a car, zooming towards you, does a quick flash of its headlights, what does that really mean? Perhaps you'd like it to mean he's going to slow down and let you out. But does it? Who knows? So it might be safest to wait and make sure.

Finally, let's give a special mention to the right indicator. It has three jobs. It can tell folk that you're moving away from the left side of the road, or that you're turning right, or that you're moving to the right.

The phrase *moving to the right* includes passing parked cars and other types of overtaking. But if you're driving in a built-up area there could be literally hundreds of cars parked about the place – they're everywhere – so you can't indicate past them all, you'd never have your right indicator off. I mean, what if there's a whole line of parked cars just before you want to turn right?

How would any following traffic be supposed to realise you were turning, if you've had your indicator on for the entire length of the street?

On the other hand, if you're forced to stop behind a parked car, to wait for oncoming traffic to pass, then wait with your right indicator on. It tells traffic behind you, as well as the oncoming traffic, that you haven't just parked badly because you're a learner. No, it tells them that you're simply waiting for a gap in traffic, to get going again. Most drivers won't overtake a car that's indicating right.

So, in built-up areas it isn't generally necessary to indicate right just to pass parked cars, unless, as I just said, you've had to stop to wait for a gap in traffic. But it is necessary to indicate right when you're passing anything that's moving, including pedestrians or cyclists. And you should also indicate right when you're passing vehicles parked on a fast road – a main road or a country lane – because it's quite rare to find parked cars on them, so following drivers might be caught out by you moving out to the right.

Last thing. Remember, your indicators are for communicating with other people. Telling them stuff. Yet other drivers are far more likely to indicate right when passing a huge lorry, one that's stopped to make a delivery – even though we can all see it perfectly – than they are to indicate around a parcel that's just fallen off the back of a van, even though nobody else can see the parcel. Why is that?

LESSON 9: DRIVING IN A QUIET RESIDENTIAL AREA

As the lesson title suggests, once you've worked through this lesson, if you're then able to practice what I've talked about, get your Supervisor to drive you over to a suitable area, a quiet housing estate or a leafy suburb, and have a drive. But then, once you've driven successfully for half-an-hour or so, get your Supervisor to drive you home again. Don't make the mistake of thinking you're ready for any busy traffic on the drive home. Give yourself a few goes around quiet roads first, give yourself time to get comfortable controlling your car before you have to start worrying too much about what other drivers are doing.

In this lesson I'll discuss:
- Priority
- Priority at junctions
- Crossing the path of oncoming traffic
- Crossroads
- White lines
- Road signs
- The General Rule
- Clearance from stationary vehicles
- Meeting other traffic
- Pedestrians at junctions

- Basic left and right turns

So, a long lesson, but if you're sitting comfortably, we'll begin with dealing with traffic situations and...

Priority

This is a really important subject. It's the number one reason for driving test fails. We're talking one test candidate in eight failing for this. So, assuming a 50% overall pass rate, that means that 25% of all test fails relate to this.

Okay, so as you approach any traffic situation, first thing, you must work out who has *right of way* – so who has *priority*. In other words, who goes first. So at traffic lights, for example, the guys with the green light have priority – they can go – while the guys on red must stop at the line and wait. Traffic lights, then, alternate priority.

On roundabouts, priority goes to the guys already on the roundabout. So here it's the traffic joining the roundabout that waits. But the guys joining the roundabout don't necessarily have to stop and wait. No, instead they have to *give way* to the traffic already on the roundabout.

Giving way means not inconveniencing the traffic that has priority in the situation you're dealing with. It means not forcing them to either steer around you or to slow down for you. Now, not giving way correctly, so you making the guy who has priority slow down for you, is considered to be a serious fault on a test – and just one serious fault means a test fail.

But, as I said, a situation where you must give way doesn't necessarily mean that you have to stop. No, the best way of dealing with a give way situation is to be driving slowly enough to be safe – so that you can stop easily, if necessary – but to keep going if the way's clear.

So, approach give-way situations thinking, *I'll probably have to stop here, but I'll hopefully be able to keep going.*

So, who has…

Priority At Junctions

Picture a T-junction on a normal two-way road in a nice quiet area – it's a junction with the usual lines painted on it – and imagine yourself facing the junction, so that the road you're on ends at the road ahead of you, at the 'T' of the junction.

Now, the road you're facing, so the one that continues through the junction, is called the *major road*, and the one you're on – because it ends at the junction – is called the *minor road*. A junction can only have one major road but it can have two-or-more minor roads.

Pulling out from the minor road onto the major road is called *emerging*. And when you're emerging you must try not to force anyone driving along the major road to slow down for you. You must give way. The major road has priority.

So the first question to ask yourself as you approach a junction is: *who's on the major road?* And if it's not you, if you're on the minor road, then you must give way to the traffic that is on the major road.

Now let's turn to the second question that you need to ask yourself at a junction: *who's turning right?*

Okay, back to our junction. So, ahead of you is the major road, with the traffic coming from both your left and right…

Now picture a driver coming from your left, along that major road, who wants to turn right into the minor road, towards you. This guy needs to…

Cross The Path Of Oncoming Traffic

And when he does turn right he must give way to any oncoming traffic before crossing their path. So, same idea, he mustn't inconvenience them, he mustn't force them to slow down for him. So, question 2 was to ask yourself who's turning right? And if the answer is that you are, then you must give way to oncoming traffic before you cross their side of the road.

So that's priority at a T-junction. But what if it's a...

Crossroads

That's a major road joined by two minor roads that are opposite one-another. So, imagine a busy crossroads with two cars coming towards each other. Both are on the major road, both want to turn right. So now what happens?

Well, we know that these two cars, as they're on the major road, have priority over any traffic waiting on either of the minor roads. That much is clear. But here both cars on the major road want to turn right, so that's more complicated because neither of them has priority over the other. They're equals. So they'll have to work it out between them as to how to get past each other.

And to complicate things even further, there are two ways they can do this. The first is to pass by going round behind each other – this is called passing *right side-to-right side* – or they could turn in front of each other – *left-to-left.*

Of the two ways of doing this, of turning right at a crossroads, right-to-right is only done very rarely. Usually cars pass in front of each other, left-to-left.

Nowadays, most crossroads are controlled by traffic lights. So the next time you're out-n-about, watch cars turning right at a traffic light junction. See where they stop to give way to on-coming traffic, and watch for whether they pass in front of each other or behind each other. Do they go left-to-left or right-to-right?

Now, sometimes junctions are unmarked, so there aren't any lines painted on the road surface. In that case, at a T-junction, the road that clearly ends at the junction would generally be considered to be the minor road. But at a crossroads it's trickier because often there's no obvious end, so no obvious major road. In this situation, there is no priority – everybody's expected to work together to get through the junction safely.

But most junctions do have…

White Lines

Let's get back to our imaginary T-junction, and the lines painted there. First there's the *hazard line*. That's the one running up the centre of either one-or-both of the roads at the junction. It's a long, broken line, with short gaps between the lines. It's there, firstly, to clearly mark-out the two sides of the road. And, secondly, a hazard line is used – funnily enough – to warn you of a hazardous area.

Here the hazard is the junction. But in town it might be a bus stop or a pedestrian crossing, and out in the countryside it might be a side road or a bend. Anyway, lines along the centre of the road work on the principal of: *the more paint, the more hazard.*

So, on a dual carriageway or one-way street, where all the traffic's moving along in the same direction, you'll find *lane lines.* These are short white lines separated by long gaps. There's very little paint being used here because these are considered to be the safest type of roads.

In two-way traffic the line up the middle of the road is called the *centre line*. It looks similar to the lane line, but has ever-so-slightly longer lines and ever-so-slightly shorter gaps because two-way traffic is ever-so-slightly more hazardous!

Sometimes in the centre of the road you'll see a *hatched area* – that's a series of diagonal lines used to keep traffic apart. *Hatching* can be used to protect traffic that's using a lane which is only for turning either left or right. Or it can be used to simply make the road seem narrower than it really is – like some kind of optical illusion – to help drivers focus on their lane. Generally, you should try not to drive on hatched areas.

On fast, open roads you will often see continuous white lines along the centre of the road. These are used for the most hazardous parts of our roads, so crests of hills, blind bends, that kind of thing. Essentially, if the line nearest to you is a continuous – or solid – white line you're in a no overtaking area. You're not allowed to cross a solid line, except in an emergency.

Okay, so that's the lines that go along the road. Now let's go back to our T-junction and talk about the lines that go across the road at the junction, the ones separating the minor road from the major road. The line going from the right of the minor road's hazard line over to the right-hand kerb is the *carriageway line*. It's a single, short, dotted line, and it's there to show the traffic on the major road where the major road's going. It's like a continuation of the major road's kerb, done in white paint.

Finally, the line going from the left of the hazard line over to the left-hand kerb is the *give way line*. It's a double dotted white line, and it's there to show the minor road traffic that they've reached the end of the line. It's saying that the road you're on is now the minor road at this junction, so the traffic on the road ahead of you has priority.

White lines, then, are one of the ways that the road communicates with you. The other way is through the use of...

Road Signs

At most T-junctions, like the one we've been picturing up to now, there aren't any signs there, just the lines painted on the road, including the give way line. But at about one give-way junction in-a-hundred, you'll also see a road sign alongside the junction in the shape of an upside-down, or inverted, triangle. This is the *end of the road* sign, used here to warn you that the junction you're approaching is especially dangerous in some way. The inverted triangle's warning you to take extra care.

And then, on around one junction in a thousand, you'll see a *stop sign*. This is the bright red octagon, the eight sided sign. The stop sign is used in conjunction with a stop line – that's a thick, solid white line, painted instead of the more common give way line.

When you reach a stop line you must stop! And that's actually stop, not just slow right down. Sounds obvious, I know, but if you don't properly stop, and a policeman sees you, it could be penalty points. And on test, if you fail to stop at a stop line… yep…it'll be a fail!

So, because both the end of road sign and the stop sign are considered to be super important, they each get their own dedicated shape. But most other signs fall into one of three family shapes. Circles give orders. Think of the letter 'O' in order. Then, further to that, red circles tell you things that you must *not* do, and blue circles tell you things that you must do.

Triangles give warnings. Take a look at the switch for a car's hazard warning lights, you'll usually see a little triangular graphic there.

And rectangles give information. Think of a text book or a college computer screen, and the rectangular shape of those.

So, to recap:

- Triangles warn
- Rectangles inform
- Circles order
- Then red circles say *don't*
- While blue circles say *do*

So, armed with this knowledge of shape and colour, you don't then need to learn every single sign in the *Highway Code*. No, you can just *read* the traffic signs. You can work-out what they mean by literally describing the little graphic shown in the middle of the sign.

So a triangle with a bicycle in the middle says *warning of bicycles up ahead.* And a red circle with a bicycle in the middle, says *don't cycle here.* While a blue circle with that same bike in it says, *do cycle – it's a cycle path.*

So signs work to a system of rules. And so do traffic lanes. They work to what we'll call...

The General Rule

And that rule – *the general rule* – says that here, in the UK, we drive on the left, unless we're turning right or overtaking. Well, usually. Say at 99% of junctions, anyway. The other 1% has a mixture of road signs and painted arrows there to make sure that we all know that at this particular junction we should ig-nore the general rule and do what the signs and arrows tell us to do instead.

So, if there aren't any arrows telling you which lane to use, assume that the left-hand lane's for turning left and going straight-ahead, as per the general rule. But if there are arrows, let them guide you as to which lane to use.

On test, your Examiner will only direct you when he wants you to make a turn. If he just wants you to go straight-ahead at a junction he simply stays quiet. So he doesn't direct you with constant instructions to *go straight-ahead*. He only directs you to make either left or right turns.

Your Examiner also won't point-out to you when a lane is arrowed for straight-ahead. You're expected to take note of the arrows and make any necessary lane changes yourself. So keep an eye out for those arrows on the approach to junctions.

The other part to the general rule says: *keep left unless you're turning right or overtaking.* So move over to the right to turn right. If there's a choice of lanes, generally use the right-hand one to turn right. But if there isn't a dedicated lane for turning right, but there is a centre white line, move across, so that you're positioned just to the left of it. However, if there isn't a centre line, then keep over to the left, even when you're turning right.

A common mistake, wherever there isn't a centre line, is for guys turning right to be too far over to the right. So don't guess where the middle of the road is. Don't guess where the centre line should be. Just stay over to the left.

And we also move over to the right to overtake. Overtaking on the left is called *undertaking* and isn't generally allowed. However, you are allowed to undertake if you're on a one-way street, or if the guy ahead of you is turning right, or if you're in, say, a traffic jam, and the left-hand lane just happens to be moving more freely than the right-hand lane.

Anyway, passing parked cars is a form of overtaking, and leads us on to another thing that your Examiner will be watching on test, known as...

Clearance From Stationary Vehicles

Clearance means finding the right balance between the distance you are from any potential danger and the speed you're doing.

So if you're able to stay a couple of metres away from, say, a row of parked cars, then you can drive at-or-around the speed limit.

Now, your Examiner won't mind you driving through a narrow gap, provided you ease through, nice-n-slowly. As I said, clearance is the balance between your distance from danger and the speed you choose.

So if you're forced-in close to parked cars by, say, oncoming traffic, then you're expected to slow right down, because you'll have nowhere else to go if things go wrong – you'll have no swerving room. Your only defence would be to stop if a door from one of those parked cars opened.

And car doors are massive! If you're looking at the front of a car as its doors open, it's like watching Dumbo's ears unfolding on the big screen! Huge things! So give them plenty of room.

When dealing with parked cars, try to move out to pass them nice-n-early. Try to pass parallel with them. So try to avoid lurching out around them at the last moment, because that'll make the front of your car swing out onto the other side of the road, meaning you'll need far more room, making your car seem much wider than it really is.

Another traffic priority situation is…

Meeting Other Traffic

When cars are parked on your side of the road, you have to give way and wait for any oncoming traffic to pass, before you pull out onto the wrong side of the road to continue on past the parked cars.

And if you do have to wait, as I talked about in Lesson 8, wait with your right indicator on, a couple of car lengths back from the parked car, and out towards the centre of the road. This gives you the best possible view along the road, and also lets other traffic know what you're waiting to do. It follows, then, that if the parked cars are on the other side of the road, then you have priority over oncoming traffic. They should wait for you.

But what about when there are parked cars on both sides of the road? Well, then neither side has priority, so it generally comes down to first-come-first-served. In other words, whoever gets there first expects to go through the gap first. But it doesn't always work like that. No, sometimes, when you're clearly going to reach the gap first – well ahead of the other guy – it becomes painfully obvious that he has no intention of waiting for you. Instead, he just moves out, aiming straight for you.

In that situation, try to think *defensively*. I mean, is it really worth a crash or an argument over a few seconds? And also, on test, if you find yourself face-to-face with some bully flying through the gap towards you, there's only one person your Examiner can fail, and that's you. So, yes…I know it can be really annoying…but just let it go.

Another priority situation is dealing with…

Pedestrians At Junctions

Think of our T-junction again. And picture the major road at the junction and the two footpaths there, one either side of it. Now consider the way the minor road meets the major road, and remember the give way line and the carriageway line painted across the face of the minor road.

Now, imagine replacing those two lines with a zebra crossing, a crossing linking those two footpaths together. Take a moment to picture it: a zebra crossing, following the course of the major road, painted across every single junction in the UK. Now, what you're picturing is the way every junction *should* work. The major road has priority through the junction and so does the major road's footpath.

So cars turning off or emerging onto the major road, should give way to pedestrians crossing the minor road using our virtual zebra crossing. But there's that word again: *should*. Drivers *should* give way to pedestrians who are crossing. But we all know – don't we? – that most car drivers completely ignore this rule. I mean, how many times have you had to dash across the road because a driver clearly has no intention of waiting for you to cross, even though you have priority?

So, after you've passed your test, don't be like them! And when you're actually on your test, if you fail to give way to those pedestrians…well, again, you fail.

It can be tricky, though. If a pedestrian's standing there, at the junction, but he doesn't start to cross, then you, in your car, have priority. But it's when they're crossing that you must wait, and let the pedestrians get to the other side of the road.

Finally, then, for this lesson, we'll round things up by talking about…

Basic Left And Right Turns

Let's start with emerging from the minor road and turning left.

Try to approach the junction keeping neatly over the left, unless there are parked cars in your way. Then, a couple of car lengths away from the junction, start working out just what you can see. If your view's good, and it looks clear of traffic, shift into 2nd gear, check that it's all clear again – and if it is – then just carry on.

But if you can see that you're going to have to give way, or your view of the junction's blocked by parked cars, or whatever, then press the clutch down, let the speed drop right down to a walking pace, and go for 1st gear instead. Then, keeping the clutch down, coast up to the junction, all the while looking left and right, making up your mind about whether or not you'll have to stop.

This is the *passive* part of your junction sequence: clutch down, coasting, looking left and right, accessing the junction, accessing the traffic. And, yes, look both ways, even when you're *only* turning left. Remember, traffic coming from your left that's out passing parked cars is likely to be on the wrong side of the road – but they're on the wrong side of the *major* road, so you still have to give way to them.

Oh, and never trust a left indicator from a car coming from your right. If you emerge, assuming he's definitely turning left, and there's a crash because – as it turns out – he didn't turn left, then the crash is considered to be your fault for pulling out, not his for indicating carelessly. Happens all the time. Maybe there's a post box just after the road you're emerging from, and that guy driving towards you keeps forgetting to post his mum's birthday card...

Anyway, when you're clear to emerge, whether or not you're stationary, move into the *positive* phase of the sequence, by releasing the brakes and easing the clutch up enough to get your engine pulling you forward again. The idea is to emerge – to cross the line – being driven forward by your engine, to not just coast onto the major road.

Then keep the clutch still while you steer. Roughly speaking, the clutch comes up at the same time as you straighten up. A lot of new drivers try to lift the clutch up within the first couple of metres of leaving the junction, while experienced drivers allow themselves a couple of car lengths before their clutch is fully up.

Now, emerging and turning right is basically the same as turning left, except, as I've said, if possible, position your car over to the right of your lane, which on a two-way street is just to the left of centre.

In both instances, when you're emerging, turning either left or right, if your view of the junction's blocked, you will have to *creep-n-peep*. Creep-n-peep! That sounds a bit dodgy! Anyway, don't panic, it just means creeping your car forward, controlling the clutch, while leaning your body forward, straining to see if the road's clear. It's only when you're sure it's clear that you can finally drive away.

Approaching a major road from a minor road, whether turning left or right, is made more difficult if you're driving uphill. This is where the holding point technique, discussed in Lesson 6, really comes into its own. The idea is to press the clutch down and coast up to the junction, losing speed, changing down into 1st gear, all the while allowing momentum to keep you rolling up to the junction. Try not to panic about rolling back. After all, if your car's moving forwards it has to stop first before it can roll back! But new drivers tend to worry that they'll just suddenly start falling backwards, down the hill.

Then, as you arrive at the junction, your speed now dropping away to a walking pace, ease the clutch back up to catch the car, just before it stops. This way you can either hold still or creep forward, ready to positively drive onto the major road. But if you're forced to stop for any more than a few seconds, or if you do start to roll back, press the clutch back down and use the foot-brake to keep you still. Then pull the handbrake on, and then when you're ready to move away again, do a normal hill-start.

The final point on emerging, is that once you've pulled out onto the major road you need to accelerate. It's not good enough on test to just pull out into an adequate gap in traffic, giving everyone plenty of room, but to then hold other drivers up by not accelerating. So there are two parts to emerging and giving way:

- First: find a big enough gap to emerge safely
- Second: when you do emerge, get your speed up nice-n-quickly

Okay, so that's emerging. Now let's talk about turning in from the major road to the minor road.

So, again, when turning left, try to keep neatly into the kerb on both the approach and the exit of the turn. Try not to wander over to the hazard line.

And turning right, try to avoid *cutting the corner*. Cutting the corner means turning in too soon and driving on the wrong side of the road. So, wait until you reach the centre of the road you're turning into – usually shown by its hazard line – before steering in. And if you have to wait for oncoming traffic to pass, wait with the front of your car in line with the minor road's hazard line.

Then, as you turn into the side road, look along its left-hand kerb to help with your steering as you straighten up. Remember, you go where you look, so look where you want to go! If you look at the hazard line as you turn in, then you're likely to drift onto the line.

Turning into a side road, either left or right, is usually done in 2nd gear. And it's also usually done with the clutch up. Changing down into 2nd, then bringing the clutch back up, gives you loads of engine braking and really helps you to keep your speed and steering under control.

But sometimes, on really tight turns, it might be necessary to use the controlled coasting technique, also from Lesson 6. This involves slowing right down, to below 10mph, but rather than changing down into 1st gear, you simply stay in 2nd but hold the clutch down, coasting around the corner, controlling your speed with the brakes if necessary. Then, as you straighten up to drive away from the junction, give the engine a bit of gas and ease the clutch back up.

Now, just before turning into a side road, take a moment to look into it through a side window, to see what's going on in the new road, to see what you're letting yourself in for. Maybe there are pedestrians crossing the road, or parked cars to nip round. But, whatever, try to avoid turning into a side road just looking solely through your windscreen. If you do, by the time you catch sight of those pedestrians or parked cars it might be too late to deal with them safely.

As for steering, as you prepare to turn, lift your hand – depending on the way you want to turn – high up on the steering-wheel, so that you can get a good initial pull down on the wheel. The idea is to steer in quickly. When you're halfway round a corner, it's much easier to take steering off than it is to put more on. Also, if you steer in quickly, it means you can be more relaxed about straightening up. You'll have more time. But if you steer in slowly, you'll find yourself playing catch-up with the steering all the way round the corner.

Okay, so a super-quick recap:

- Remember to use your mirrors
- Remember to carefully time your indicators
- Remember to watch for pedestrians
- Remember that Examiners are in no hurry, so take your time

Okay, well this has been a marathon lesson, but let's end by boiling pretty much everything we've covered down into four words:

- Mirror
- Signal
- Speed
- Gear

So the way it works: check your mirrors as you approach a hazard or a junction. Think about the timing of any signals you intend to give. Slow down. Change down.

And one final thought: ***Examiners are slow to fail people who drive too slow, but quick to fail people who drive too quick***. So remember to take your time.

LESSON 10: ROUNDABOUTS

I hope that if you were able to have some practice drives after Lesson 9 that they went well, not too stressful! Now, in this lesson, I'll start by talking about the system of lanes and signals, and also priority at roundabouts, then we'll move onto:

- Putting it all into practice
- The test
- Mini-roundabouts

Let's get started.

A roundabout, then, is essentially a small one-way system with a flowerbed in the middle! The road going around the flowerbed is the major road. The roads joining the roundabout are minor roads (except on some very rare occasions when priority's given to traffic approaching the roundabout and staying in its lane). So, in all but a tiny number of cases, priority goes to traffic already on the roundabout.

So even if you've been driving along a main road for miles, when you meet a roundabout your road becomes the minor road, and you must give way to traffic coming round from your right.

To choose your lane and road position approaching the roundabout, use the general rule that we discussed in Lesson 9. So, keep left unless you're turning right or overtaking, or where painted arrows show otherwise. Also, indicate on the approach if you're planning on turning either left or right, but, same as other junctions, you don't need to indicate if you're going straight-ahead.

So, approaching a roundabout, lanes and signals work in the same way as they do for any other type of junction.

But where roundabouts do differ from other junctions, is that on roundabouts you signal twice. Once, as I said, as you approach, and then again as you leave the roundabout. The rule here is that you always exit a roundabout indicating left. So it doesn't matter where you've come from or where you're going to – in all but a very few cases – indicate left as you exit.

You see, leaving a roundabout, but not indicating left is a real pain for other drivers. That simple left indicator, that takes virtually no effort whatsoever on our part, is to tell waiting drivers that you're leaving, letting them know they can take your place. It's a courtesy indicator, good manners! But if you don't indicate, those other drivers stop, because they're not sure where you're going, which in turn stops the drivers behind them, lengthening the queues, lengthening the time it takes us all to get home at night.

Now, you may have noticed that, like other junctions, roundabouts are not always black-n-white. They vary. And in your area, and the area in which you'll be taking your test, there's going to be one-or-two roundabouts that aren't necessarily clear-cut, where you're going to have to pull over and discuss how to deal with them with your Supervisor.

But, bearing that in mind, this is a run down of how roundabouts generally work:

- Turning Left, the 1st exit:
- Approach in the left lane, indicating left
- Keep to the left as you emerge onto the roundabout
- Keep your left indicator on as you leave
- *

- Going straight-ahead, 2nd exit:
- Approach in the left lane, no indicator
- Keep to the left as you emerge
- Indicate left as you pass the road before the one you're taking
- Leave by the left lane, indicating left
- *

- Turning Right, 3rd exit:
- Approach in the right lane, indicating right
- Emerge onto the right lane
- Indicate left as you pass the road before the one you're taking
- Change lanes, exiting in the left lane, left indicator

Remember, though, that the general rule says that at junctions you can use the right-hand lane to overtake, as well as using it for turning right, and that's the same here, at roundabouts. So, if a roundabout has two lanes going straight-ahead on the approach, and two on the exit, it's usually okay to use the right-hand lane as an overtaking lane. In that case, you indicate in the same way as you would for straight-ahead – so, no indicator on the approach, then a left indicator for the exit – and simply use the right-hand lane throughout.

Incidentally, the sign that you see as you approach a roundabout should give you an indication of whether-or-not there'll be an overtaking lane on the exit. The thickness of the lines showing the various exits from the roundabout *should* tell you how many lanes there will be. So a thin line, one lane. A thick line, two lanes. But I said that's how it should work because those lines aren't always marked correctly.

Okay. Now let's talk a little bit about roundabouts in a more practical sense. And let's begin at the beginning, by talking about the approach.

If possible, sort your lane out nice-n-early and if necessary use the *breaking the signal* technique. So that's one indicator for any lane change – switch it off for a few seconds – then indicate a second time for the roundabout itself.

Then, engine braking. So come off the gas to let your engine settle the car down. This will make the approach more relaxed and controlled, rather than just flying up and going from gas to brake in a mad panic.

Next, the gear. If you're joining the back of a queue, just pop 1st gear in as you arrive. But if you think it might be possible to keep going at the roundabout, then change down into 2nd just before you reach the point where the road kicks round to the left, just before the roundabout itself. Then you'll be able to use controlled coasting – so, clutch down, controllin' the rollin' with the brake – for the last couple of car lengths, as you look for your chance to join the roundabout.

But keep an eye on the car in front of you. No, seriously! It's one of our most common crashes: running into the guy in front of you at a roundabout. Happens all the time. And it's such a common crash simply because drivers are looking for a gap in traffic – and driving off when they spot one – before the guy in front's even moved.

So make sure the guy in front has definitely moved away before you look to the right, before you start looking for your gap.

And even if the road ahead of you is clear as you approach the roundabout – there's no-one there at all – still watch where you're going. Remember, you go where you look. If you spend all your time looking to your right then you'll move to your right, out of your lane.

So take your time and split where you're looking between your windscreen – to keep your steering accurate – and your side window, watching your zone.

Oh, what's this *zone*, I hear you ask? Well, the zone in question is the bit of the roundabout to your immediate right. So, if you imagine a roundabout like a clock face – and you're approaching from six o'clock – then the zone we're talking about is the bit that goes round anticlockwise to three o'clock. That's the area we're interested in. That's your zone. And the guys in your zone have priority.

So how do you get onto the roundabout – it all looks so busy – when's it your turn?

There are three things you're watching for:

- A clear zone
- One car in the zone but it's indicating left
- A gap that you can move into, either before or after a car in the zone

Okay. Let's run through those three.

First: a clear zone. Fairly self-explanatory, I suppose, but notice a clear zone doesn't necessarily mean there's no traffic at all to your right. There could be cars waiting to join the roundabout from the road over to your right. But they're still waiting to join the roundabout. They're not actually on it yet. Remember, your zone refers to the roundabout itself. It doesn't include the roads leading up to the roundabout.

Second: there's a car in the zone but it's indicating left. So you have a driver who's very kindly letting you know that he's leaving the roundabout before he reaches you, letting you know that you can take his place.

And finally, three: moving into a gap. Okay, picture one of those luggage carousels at an airport, the things you pick your cases up from after a flight. Now imagine it was your job to load all the bags from the plane onto the conveyor belt. You've had a tough day, you're tired, but this is the last flight you have to unload, and you've now got just one more case to put on the conveyor before you finish work for the day. But the conveyor's full. Still, never mind, here come the passengers, and the conveyor starts to move. Now, are you watching the bags as they trundle past you, or are you looking for a gap to put this last case into?

Well, a roundabout's like that. Try not to just stare at the traffic. Instead, look for a gap to move into. So look behind the car to your right – for a gap – and not directly at it. At busy times of the day, getting onto a roundabout is all about looking for a suitable gap. If you want it to be completely clear then you could be in for a long wait!

So, to recap:

- Don't worry about those cars waiting to join the roundabout from the road over to your right. Those guys are the same as you. They're still on the minor road. They don't have priority over you until they move onto the roundabout and into your zone

- Don't worry about that guy in your zone, the one who's indicating left. He's telling you that he's leaving your zone before he reaches you

- Don't worry about that one lonely car on an otherwise deserted roundabout, the one now in your zone, because, with careful timing, you can join the roundabout immediately behind him, without having to stop

But one final word about your zone. And that is, notice that we're *not* talking about lanes here, because the zone is *all the lanes to your right*. So, if you're turning left, don't fall into the trap of only looking at the lane nearest to you, thinking of it as *your* lane. Because it isn't. A driver turning right, using the lane nearest the roundabout, can change lanes and move across towards you at any moment. Remember, he's already on the roundabout, so it's his lane – if he wants it – not yours.

Now let's talk about the way your Examiner will direct you as you approach roundabouts on test. So, he might say, 'At the roundabout, I'd like you to turn left. That's the first exit, sign-posted London.' Or, he might say, 'At the roundabout, I'd like you to go straight-ahead. That's the second exit, sign-posted Glasgow.'

So you're given nice clear directions. But if you still find yourself feeling unsure about where you're going, it's okay for you to ask your Examiner to repeat the direction, or even to ask for further clarification if you need more detail. Whatever, it's important that you're clear in your own mind exactly where you're going *before* you get onto the roundabout.

But you're not being tested on your ability to follow directions. So if you do make a mistake on test, and you realise you're in the wrong lane, then try not to worry about it. Simply go wherever the lane you're in leads you. Provided you signal correctly for the direction that you're now going in, you won't be marked down. However, you will be marked down if, on realising your mistake, you attempt some kind of crazy last-minute lane-change.

Now, mirrors, as you know, are a really big deal on test. So it's obviously important to use the mirrors correctly on roundabouts. Firstly, use the mirror, signal, manoeuvre routine as you approach a roundabout. Then, on the roundabout itself, again, use the mirrors before indicating left, to leave.

When you're turning right, and you reach the point where you need to start your lane change – to move from the right-hand lane over to your left – you've got a whole lot to do! Your Examiner wants to see that you:

- Check your rear-view mirror
- Switch your indicators from right to left
- Use your left-hand door mirror

- Glance to your left-hand blind-spot

…and all in those few seconds!

Finally a quick word about…

Mini Roundabouts

These are the small ones – funnily enough – that are simply a painted circle on the road. They have an additional sign that you'll see on the approach, a blue circle showing three arrows arranged around it. This sign's telling you that you must drive around the painted circle, not over it or on the wrong side of it.

Another road-sign you'll often see when approaching a mini-roundabout is a simple written one that says, *give way to the right*. The reason for this is that, as you know, on a full-sized roundabout you give way to traffic on the roundabout, in your zone. But on a mini-roundabout you also need to be wary of traffic *approaching* the roundabout, because often those guys will approach really quickly, flying onto the mini roundabout, which means they'll be right on top of you in no time at all. So, be super careful, and take a moment to look a bit further down the road, rather than simply focusing on your zone.

Signalling also differs on a mini-roundabout compared to a full-sized one because you only need to indicate for a mini-round-about on the approach to it. They're so tight there usually isn't time to indicate left as you're leaving it, even after a right turn.

Okay, so that's the end of the roundabout lesson. Like every-thing else in this driving lark, take your time. It sounds like a contradiction, but if you approach roundabouts slowly you'll ac-tually get around them quicker because you won't need to stop as often.

So, approach carefully, watch out for the guy in front of you, and try to work out what's happening in your zone.

LESSON 11:
TRAFFIC LIGHTS

In this lesson we're first going to be discussing priority at traffic lights, then we'll move onto:

- Sequence
- Filter arrows and filter lanes
- Slip lanes
- Pedestrian crossings
- Sensors
- Turning right
- Turning left

The purpose of traffic lights is to alternate priority at busy junctions. So the guys with the green light have priority, the ones on red wait. Then the lights change and it swaps round. Then the lights change again and now the pedestrians get their turn, and so on.

When you're approaching traffic lights use the general rule that we first discussed in lesson 9. So keep to the left unless you're turning right or overtaking, except where road arrows show otherwise. And on test, remember that your Examiner will only direct you at lights if he wants you to turn either left or right. He won't tell you to go straight-ahead. He'll expect you to do that for yourself. So, when you're out practising, remind your Supervisor to keep quiet at lights, unless he wants you to turn.

As you approach a green light, be prepared for them to change.

Traffic lights don't change suddenly, they just change. It's what they do! So be ready. But that doesn't necessarily mean you need to slow down. Being ready can sometimes just be a mental preparation thing. In thirty limits it's usually okay to stay at a constant speed, but to just keep one eye on the lights. Slowing down when the lights are still at green will just irritate following traffic, causing them to get even closer to your back bumper than they already are.

Okay, now let's talk about...

Sequence

It goes:

- Green
- Amber
- Red
- Red and Amber
- Green

So, let's fill in some detail, and let's start with green. Green means go. Everybody knows that. Ah...but it means go, provided there's *somewhere to go*. It doesn't just mean pull forward into a queue and block the junction. So if there's a traffic jam ahead of you, wait behind the white line until there's enough room to cross the junction fully.

Next is amber. Amber on its own. Amber means stop. It *doesn't* mean prepare to stop. But it doesn't mean panic, and do some wild emergency stop, either. Amber means stop provided you can stop safely before you reach the line. But if you feel as though you can't stop safely then it's okay to keep going. That's what amber's for.

Sometimes, when guys get stopped by a nice policeman who tells them that he saw them *jump the lights*, they reply that the lights were *only* amber. This tells the nice policeman that they don't actually know what the amber light means. Maybe, if instead they said: *I saw the lights were at amber but I didn't think I could stop safely in time*, then our nice policeman might be more forgiving!

Anyway, amber is on for a couple of seconds and is followed by red. Red means stop. Stop before the line. It's illegal, so you'd fail your test, to cross the line on red. Notice that the white line here is a solid line, a *stop line*, not just a give way line.

When you're waiting at red, keep still – so none of this creeping forward lark. And wait with your handbrake on and the gears in neutral.

Next is red and amber together. That's get ready to go. Again, it's on for just a couple of seconds. Bit of a waste of time, this one. In fact, in some countries they don't bother with it at all, they just go directly from red to green. Which, in a way, kind of makes sense. I mean, if red and amber together means *get ready to go* it's no wonder some drivers think amber on its own means *get ready to stop*.

Anyway…green, amber, red, red and amber together, green. That's your sequence. So if you see amber on its own then next is going to be red.

Now, at some lights, as well as the three main lights I've just talked about, you'll see another light alongside green, making an 'L' shape. These are…

Filter Arrows And Filter Lanes

Filter arrows are additional green lights, a little bonus green light. When there's a left filter arrow there will also be a left filter lane – a separate lane with a turn left arrow painted on the road.

Left filter arrows usually come on while the main light is still at red, allowing just the traffic turning left to go. The green filter arrow then stays on until the main lights change to green. At that point, the filter's no longer needed because when the main green light is on everybody facing the light can go – so those going straight-ahead and right, as well as left.

A mistake learners often make, approaching traffic lights, is that they see the left filter arrow come on but then continue watching just that one light – the green arrow – as they approach the junction. So then, if the arrow goes out they stop, because they've been so focused on that filter arrow that they haven't noticed that the main green has come on! So it's the red light coming on that tells you to stop, not the green arrow simply going out.

Filter arrows to the right come on either after or with the main green. It's there to tell you that the oncoming traffic now has a red light – so they should stop – allowing you to turn right. Right filter arrows don't always have their own lane. Sometimes you share with traffic going straight ahead.

And sometimes at traffic lights there's a separate lane for turning left just before you reach the white stop line. These are...

Slip Lanes

...and they take you away from the main traffic light junction and bring you to their own junction instead. Usually slip lanes end in a give way line, but sometimes they have their own, separate, traffic light. And sometimes they have a traffic-light-controlled pedestrian-crossing halfway down them, followed by a give way line. When slip lanes do end in a give way line, give way to traffic coming from the main junction, which is now to your right.

Slip lanes help keep things flowing by allowing traffic to turn left even when the main junction light is at red. Which is a good thing. But a bad thing is that sometimes pedestrians casually cross the slip lane, mistakenly assuming that when the green man, on the main junction, is on that it also protects the slip lane. But it doesn't. Not necessarily. The slip lane is separate from the main junction.

All of which brings us neatly onto...

Pedestrians

If you look at the white stop line at the junction, you'll see that just after it there are usually two rows of metal studs set into the road surface. They mark the pedestrian crossing area. Most traffic light junctions have a pedestrian crossing across each of its roads, so a crossroads usually has four crossings.

The idea is that, when someone presses the crossing button at the junction, the computer controlling the lights will, at some point during its cycle, stop all the traffic with red lights then light-up the green man. And the pedestrians cross.

So is the green man just for the pedestrians, and has nothing to do with the drivers? No. Okay, so when the green man's on, then all the traffic is stopped at red. But what about if a driver's in the middle of the junction, waiting to turn right, when his light turned red and the green man came on?

Well, then it would be up to him to have seen that the green man has come on and give way to any pedestrians who are crossing. So, yes, you do need to keep an eye on the green man, as well as the main traffic lights.

Now, as I've said, the pedestrian's green man only comes on if someone's pressed the button. The button sends a signal to the computer controlling the lights, letting it know somebody wants to cross. Well, as you approach the traffic lights in your car, you press a kind of button, too. Or, at least, your car does. Because as you roll up to the lights, you drive across a series of...

Sensors

...which are laid into the road surface, sending signals to the computer, letting it know that you've arrived at the junction. You'll see them as lines of shiny tarmac starting ten-to-fifteen metres back from the stop line. They can look as if they're just scars leftover from long-finished road-works. Every road approaching every traffic light junction has them, at least three sets of them, constantly updating the computer about the flow of traffic.

So traffic lights don't just change randomly. You'll see this most clearly if you approach a red light at four o'clock in the morning. Then, provided you're not speeding, as you arrive at the lights they'll be changing to green for you, good as gold. Four in the afternoon, however, is a different story. The dreaded school run is in full swing and the poor computer's struggling to keep things moving. So eventually it becomes overwhelmed and goes into a default mode of, say, sixty seconds for this road then sixty seconds for the other road.

Right filter arrows, as I've already said, sometimes come on simultaneously with the main green. But at other junctions they come on after the main green has been on for a while, allowing the cars waiting to turn right to go. At these junctions, there's an additional sensor immediately after both the white line and the pedestrian crossing. It's usually the size and shape of a living-room rug, and its job is to tell the computer that the right turn traffic is building up. So, effectively, it switches the right green-filter-arrow on.

So, when you're sitting first in the queue, waiting at red, waiting to turn right – and you can see that the lights have that distinctive 'L' shape – look at the road surface ahead of you to see if there's an additional sensor there. Then, if there is one, when the lights change to green and you move forward, if the filter arrow hasn't come on, wait right there, right on top of that sensor, letting the computer know that you're waiting for the arrow to help you turn.

But, what about if you're...

Turning Right

...and there isn't a green filter arrow? Well, we started this lesson talking about priority, and the way traffic lights alternate priority. So at lights, the road with the green light is the major road. But remember, there are two priority rules at junctions. In Lesson 9, I talked about the two questions you should ask yourself about priority as you approach a junction. The first related to the major road. So here, as I've said, that means the road with the green light. But the second question was: who's turning right? And this second rule also comes into play here, at traffic lights.

So a green light gives you permission to enter the junction. But if you're turning right, you must still give way to oncoming traffic. So when you get the green light, pull forward to the other side of the pedestrian crossing area and, if there's oncoming traffic, that's where you wait.

And you're waiting for one of three things:
- A gap in the oncoming traffic
- Your light going back to red and the oncoming traffic stopping
- Or, if there is one, a green right-turn filter-arrow

And, of course, the fourth thing to watch out for, as we discussed a moment ago, is for any pedestrians using the crossing area that you'll be driving across as you make your turn.

Once you've crossed the white line and positioned yourself for the right turn, you're committed now to completing the turn. So, even if your light turns red, you're expected to finish your turn, to clear the junction, to get out of the way, ideally before the next line of traffic starts moving. So, yes, you need your wits about you. From your light changing to red, to the next line of traffic moving away again on green, is only five-or-six seconds. That's all the time you've got.

The good news, though, is that…

Turning Left

…is easier.

The main thing is to watch for cyclists. They'll sneak up between you and the kerb and might not notice your indicator. Ah…indicators. I mean, why do so many drivers wait until the lights change to green, and they're moving again, before they indicate? The indicators are to tell people what you're going to do *next*, not what you're doing *now*. Sticking an indicator on the split-second before turning left is no use to anyone. And remember, that includes when you're in a lane which only goes in one direction.

Anyway, let's end this lesson telling you something that you already know. That jumping lights is pretty much the most dangerous habit you can get into. So don't be an *amber gambler*, as the TV advert-thing used to say. But some drivers do choose to take that risk. They start by casually driving past amber lights, usually when they're leading a line of traffic. Then they move onto passing other drivers who were ahead of them but have chosen to stop. Before, finally – and, in some cases, I really do mean *finally* – graduating onto *they've only just changed to red so I've still got ages yet.*

It always goes wrong eventually.

LESSON 12: CITY CENTRES

In this lesson I'll be discussing:

- Lane changing
- Tricks of the Trade
- Speed bumps
- Pedestrian crossings

City traffic is like a game of chess. The pieces move in different ways to different rules at different beats. Each piece has strengths and weaknesses, yet each moves easily, keeping the game flowing.

For drivers, keeping that flow is all about knowing the correct lane to be in – and being in it nice-n-early. It's the key to a stress-free city-life. But maybe you're a stranger in town; so maybe it's not that easy. And if that is the case, then take it slow.

And keep looking. Direction signs can be lost in the sea of glass and neon, but they are there. So look even further ahead than normal, especially while you're stationary, and search them out.

Oh, and remember that busy city centre routes are often one-way systems, and that on a one-way system traffic can be passing you on either side. There's no overtaking lane on a one-way street.

Also, whether you're new here or a regular, get used to sharing. Sharing road space, sharing time. Sometimes other drivers will wait for you; sometimes you'll wait for other drivers. Sit back and let things sort themselves out in front of you. Let other drivers do their thing. You can't hurry them.

But, even if you're chilled out, heavy traffic can still feel overwhelming. Lots of lanes, lots of metal. If you feel your stress levels rising, try to focus on your immediate area. Focus on your lane, keeping to the centre of it, keeping well back from the car in front. I mean, no matter how heavy the traffic, no matter how many lanes there are, it's really only the car directly ahead of you that's your immediate concern.

Now, to keep your car moving smoothly in heavy traffic, picture a boy kicking his football along the path alongside you. He gives it a little kick and the ball rolls...then another little kick.

You do a similar thing with your car. Ease the clutch up and give the car a little kick with the engine. Then, when the brake lights ahead of you flash on again, press your clutch down and coast. Let your car roll for a bit. Maybe you need the brake, maybe you don't. Then clutch up again...another kick. There's nothing wrong with using controlled coasting. There's nothing wrong with pressing the clutch down before the brake when you're in first gear.

And there's nothing wrong with...

Changing Lanes

When you're changing lanes you must give way to the guys already in the lane you want to move into. But just like emerging from a side street, that doesn't mean you have to wait for someone to let you in. No, moving over is fine, provided you don't force other drivers to brake or swerve.

So, for a lane change, check your mirrors, pop an indicator on, a quick blind-spot glance, then ease over towards the white line, just to let the other drivers know you want to move across. This is a driver's version of assertive body language: being positive without being aggressive.

When you're positive in this way, other drivers will be more likely to let you in. But if you're either too timid – shying away from the white line – or too aggressive – veering across onto the white line – then you've got no chance. The traffic will close up and you'll be ignored.

And turning into side streets, especially if you're having to cross either a bus or cycle lane, watch for cyclists whizzing up on your left, or even threading between lanes of cars. Use those door mirrors. Use those blind-spot checks. Don't make snap decisions.

Anyway, in heavy traffic, if you're having trouble changing lanes or pulling out of a side street, you could do worse than try a couple of the...

Tricks Of The Trade

...used by crafty old lorry-drivers. The first is to try and seek out eye-contact with passing drivers. A truck driver, stuck in a side road, will wind his window down and look directly at the passing queue of car drivers from the cab of his big, slow lorry. Of course, the car drivers don't want to let him into their lane, they don't want to be stuck behind him, so they'll pretend not to notice him. But, eventually, he'll catch a car driver's eye, and that reluctant driver will let the lorry in. Works every time!

Traffic's an impersonal thing, everyone in their own metal box, their own suit of armour. But if you establish eye contact with a fellow driver, that armour's stripped away. You become just two people again. Two individuals.

Another technique, to help you get out of a busy side street, is to look for gaps in traffic rather than just at the traffic it-self. I touched on this in Lesson 11, talking about getting onto a roundabout, and this possibly sounds obvious, but it's easy to fall into the trap of just watching traffic flowing past you, like a river.

And watch both sides of the street, your head swivelling from side to side. Say to yourself: *there's a gap after the blue car to the left...there's a gap after the red van to the right*, and when those two gaps coincide...you're off. So don't just stare at traffic, say, from your right until there's a gap *then* look to your left. You might have just missed a chance to go, and, if not, by the time you're mentally up-to-speed again with the traffic coming from your left, the situation from your right will have changed again. So, pretend you're watching tennis – Wimbledon – your head turning rhythmically, left to right, keeping score.

In town, sometimes your view's going to be blocked by, say, a parked delivery van. When that happens, there's no point sitting at the give way line, unable to see a thing. You're going to have to use that *creep-n-peep* technique. Creeping forward, super care-fully, using the clutch, so that you can peep around the obstacle.

Think of the give way line as bending out, moulding itself around the van, with you going out to it, edging the car forward while leaning your body forward, but not committing yourself to finally going until you can see around the van, and you can see that the road's clear.

To help you as you creep-n-peep, you can use reflections from car bodywork or shop windows to help you catch a glimpse of movement from approaching traffic. And sometimes you'll catch sight of movement from shadows or from feet moving beneath vans and buses. Children getting off a school bus and crossing in front of it, or van drivers checking addresses as they walk round in front of you.

Oh, and another trick – this one for busy roundabouts – is to use busses and other long vehicles as shields when you're emerging. If there's a bus to your right, waiting at the roundabout, when it moves off you can go with it. Nothing's going to come through the bus, so as long as you keep up with it as it pulls away, you'll be fine.

A word of caution, though: this trick doesn't work with those big 4x4s. They're tall, yes, but not long enough – and way too fast – for this trick to work!

But what you can do to help against those tall cars – those 4x4s and the like – is to sit back a little bit at junctions and look along the road from behind them. With most cars, if they're along-side you, you can look through them. But not with those guys, not unless you're in one yourself. So hold back to get a view of the road, then, when you're clear, ease forward for a final check around the front of them before moving away.

Then, in the side streets, you'll see guys accelerating up to...

Speed Bumps

...then braking, going over them at walking pace, then accelerating again, up to the next one. This just puts unnecessary wear-n-tear on the brakes and tyres, and wastes fuel.

Also, when you brake, the front of your car dips down slightly because the weight of the car is transferred forward, pressing down on the front suspension. So braking at a speed bump uses up all the spring in your suspension, making the bump feel much harsher than it really is.

So, when you meet a speed bump, ideally you want to be off the brakes, but travelling slow enough to go over it smoothly. In fact, the best way of dealing with speed bumps is to drive over them, your engine gently pulling you over, with careful use of the accelerator.

The trick, for a nice smooth ride – and one that's just as quick from A-to-B – is to keep a steady speed along the length of the road, allowing your suspension to soak-up speed bumps, going easy on both the accelerator and the brakes in between.

In town, you've also got a whole bunch of...

Pedestrian Crossings

...to deal with.

There are zebra crossings, of course, though they seem to be being slowly phased out. As are pelican crossings. These are traffic-light controlled pedestrian crossings where the lights work through a slightly different sequence to normal traffic lights.

They go:

- Green
- Amber
- Red
- **Flashing amber**
- Green

At pelican crossings both the red and flashing amber phases last for around ten seconds. So as you approach the crossing you can literally countdown 10, 9, 8...

On the flashing amber phase, the rule is to stop for any pedestrians who are actually crossing, even if they're not directly in front of you. You have to wait for the crossing to be completely clear before you move on. But you don't have to wait for the green light. You can go on the flashing amber, as long as the crossing's clear.

Puffin and Toucan crossings are the newer designs. They use

sensors mounted on top of the lights to *watch* people using the crossings, then change accordingly. So it's harder to judge when they'll change back to green for you.

Puffin crossings are for pedestrians but Toucan crossings are for both pedestrians and cyclists – which is why they're remembered by thinking *two* – as in the number two – *can cross*. Two-can cross. On all traffic light crossings, and traffic lights in general, as you slow down approaching the back of a queue of traffic, don't start to accelerate the moment you see the lights up ahead change to green. It takes a couple of seconds for each vehicle to react to the one in front of it moving. So if there are ten stationary cars between you and the lights, it might take twenty seconds before the car directly in front of you starts to move. Think of the traffic moving off in the same way as a row of dominoes fall – one after another – and time your approach accordingly.

And have you noticed the zigzag lines painted either side of pedestrian crossings? They have two rules:

- No parking
- No overtaking the vehicle nearest the crossing

So if you're approaching a pedestrian crossing on, say, a two-lane one-way street, and the crossing seems to be clear, it's tempting to overtake a row of vehicles sitting there, stationary, in the other lane.

But what if the reason they're sitting there is because of one last pedestrian who's now crossing in front of the traffic. And what if the vehicle at the head of the queue is a van, a van big enough to block your view of that one last pedestrian until he pops out, right in front of you. Nightmare.

Now, your Examiner will get nervous if you get close to any pedestrians during your test, so give them plenty of room and slow down if they're crossing in front of you. But remember that the *Highway Code* says to not actually wave pedestrians across the road. The danger is that the pedestrian might think that the traffic has stopped. But you're not *the* traffic, not all of it, you're just one car, but – children especially – don't think of it like that. So don't wave them across the road and then expect them to look in the other direction. Chances are they won't.

Finally, watch for pedestrians walking between stationary cars. Your lane might be moving, but if the lane alongside you isn't, pedestrians will come marching through, possibly still focused on their phones.

LESSON 13: DUAL CARRIAGEWAYS

In this lesson I'll talk about:

- Lane discipline
- Undertaking
- Following distances
- Slip lanes
- Junctions

But first: what is a dual carriageway? Well, it's a road that isn't a motorway but looks a bit like one! *Dual* here means two, and *carriageway* means a strip of tarmac. So a dual carriageway has two strips of tarmac, running parallel with each other, with a barrier between them.

This barrier, also like a motorway, is often a strip of grass and is called a *central reservation*. And dual carriageways also, again, same as a motorway, often have an emergency lane, a *hard shoulder*.

And, on both dual carriageways and motorways, the national speed limit is 70mph, although, sometimes other speed limits are in force.

Route signs on dual carriageways are much the same as on other main roads. So green backgrounds to show the towns and cities that are further along the road, and white background signs for local destinations. Motorways use blue signs. So countdown markers on dual carriageways, for example, have white diagonal stripes on a green background. Motorways have white on blue. For both, though, each diagonal stripe represents 100 yards to, say, an exit slip-road.

Dual carriageways, again, like motorways, are described by counting the lanes in each carriageway. So, a dual carriageway, divided by a lane-line into two lanes, is called a two-lane dual carriageway.

The main difference, though, is that dual carriageways often have normal give way style junctions, including right turns and roundabouts. Motorways don't. Motorways use slip lanes positioned over to the far left-hand side of the road to both leave and join them, a system that dual carriageways also often use.

The left-hand lane on a dual carriageway is often known as the slow lane, and the lane over to the right, the one closest to the central reservation, is known as the fast lane. And then, if there are three lanes, the middle one's called the...middle lane! Ah, but all the lanes have the same speed limit, so there isn't really either a slow lane or a fast lane. The left-hand lane's for anybody to use, while the right lane's for cars both overtaking and positioning for turning right. So the lanes are more accurately described by numbering them. The left lane, then, the slow lane, is Lane 1. The lanes to the right of Lane 1 are then numbered accordingly... Lane 2, Lane 3...

Learner drivers in Great Britain are allowed on both dual carriageways and motorways. But whereas you can drive on dual carriageways with your Supervisor, you must be accompanied by an Approved Driving Instructor to practice on motorways. If you're taken onto a dual carriageway by your Examiner, and if conditions allow, you'll be expected to drive up towards the speed limit.

However, at the time of writing, if you're in Northern Ireland you're not allowed to drive on motorways at all, and on other roads, including dual carriageways, your maximum speed limit is just 45mph.

Now, also on test, if you find yourself catching up with a slower moving vehicle, and, again, conditions allow, you'll be expected to overtake. That'll mean moving over a lane to your right. The trick is to move over nice-n-early. If you do that, you're more likely to be able to keep up a nice steady speed for the lane change. But if you wait until you're virtually on top of the slower vehicle before moving out, then you'll often be forced to slow down by cars that are overtaking *you*.

So, to move into the overtaking lane, use your mirrors carefully, especially your right door mirror. Then, when you're ready to make your move, indicate. Try to plan on having your indicators flash at least three times before you change lanes. Then glance to your blind spot, for a final check.

Try to avoid treating lane changes as something you need to slow down for. Try not to lift off the accelerator and let your speed fade away. Okay, yes, sometimes it is necessary to slow down to merge with passing traffic, but generally speaking, lane changing is something best done at a constant speed.

As you overtake, focus on staying in the centre of your lane until you can see the front of the vehicle you've overtaken in your mirrors. Then indicate left, and, if all's good, move back into your original lane.

And moving back to the left, back to Lane 1, so getting out of the way of overtaking traffic, is known as having good...

Lane Discipline

But, generally speaking, our lane disciple, here in the UK, is terrible! Unlike our European neighbours, we have this *fast lane* mentality. They overtake then move immediately back into Lane 1. We don't. We like to hog the fast lane!

Anyway, on test, use the general rule, so keep to the left, keep to Lane 1, unless you're turning right or overtaking, except where road arrows tell you to do otherwise.

So, drive in Lane 1, move into Lane 2 to overtake, but then, after overtaking, move back into Lane 1. So, overtake on the right, because overtaking on the left is known as...

Undertaking

...and undertaking's illegal unless the driver ahead of you is turning right, or you're in slow traffic and Lane 1 is moving more freely than Lane 2.

The other time you're allowed to pass on the left is, as we talked about in Lesson 12, on a one-way street, so not something to really concern you here.

But what does concern you, what your Examiner will be watching for on test, is that you're in the correct lane while driving normally and overtaking, and also that you're aware of the rules for both lane discipline and undertaking.

The other thing your Examiner's going to be watching closely is your...

Following Distances

Have you ever heard the phrase, *only a fool breaks the two-second rule*? No? But I bet your Supervisor has. It used to be on the TV, in the ad breaks, all the time back-in-the-day.

The idea is that, as the vehicle you're following passes some easily identifiable landmark – a slip lane or a side road – you literally say to yourself, nice-n-slowly, *one thousand and one, one thousand and two...* and see if you're then passing that same spot in the road. If you are, you're roughly two seconds back from the guy you're following. You're obeying the two-second rule.

That two second gap is considered to be the minimum safe following distance for speeds over 40mph on dry roads. On test, if you get any closer, your Examiner will ask you to drop back. And you don't want to hear that – oh no – hearing that would almost certainly mean a test fail.

In the wet, you're supposed to double the gap and leave four seconds between you and the guy you're following. And in ice and snow, theory test questions suggest leaving a gap ten times greater than normal. Although, how you're supposed to put that into practice is anyone's guess!

Anyway, now we're going to talk about the different ways of joining and leaving dual carriageways, and we'll start with...

Slip Lanes

...and the main thing to remember, which is that, as much as possible, try to adjust your speed on the actual slip lane, not on the dual carriageway itself. The slip lanes are acceleration and deceleration lanes, so it's in them that, as much as possible, you should adjust your speed.

So, joining a carriageway, try to speed up along the slip lane before joining the main road, to lessen the speed differential between you and the traffic already on the carriageway as much as possible. If you drive slowly down an acceleration lane then it can be scary trying to join the faster road. The difference in speeds between you and the other traffic can be really intimidating, making it difficult to judge when there's a suitable gap for you to move into.

So use the acceleration lane as the name suggests, and *accelerate*. Then use your door mirror and indicate right. And, because you'll often be at an acute angle to the carriageway, check your blind-spot two-or-three times, as well, to give you the best possible view of the traffic you're planning on merging with.

But, unfortunately, if you reach the end of the slip lane, so if you reach the carriageway line, and you haven't yet been able to join the main carriageway, then you have a problem because the traffic already on the carriageway has priority so you must give way. Generally, then, in that situation, you'd have to stop and wait. But because that would put you in a dangerous position, if there is a hard shoulder it's probably best to continue on down there – steady speed, right indicator on – watching your door mirror for a gap.

When you're leaving a carriageway via a slip lane, try to keep your speed up as much as possible on the main road itself. The idea is to do the bulk of your braking, and any gear changing, in the deceleration slip lane after you've left the dual carriageway, to get yourself clear of the guys zooming up behind you.

It's really dangerous to slow down unexpectedly and unnecessarily when traffic behind you could easily be doing 70mph. And it's doubly dangerous when you're turning right, because you'll be using what – as I've already said – some drivers consider to be the *fast lane*. Unfortunately, it doesn't seem to occur to some of the fast guys out there that other people use the right-hand lane to turn right!

Also, plan the timing of your indicators. Indicate nice-n-early when you're leaving a carriageway, at least a good few seconds before you begin slowing down. And when you're turning right, remember to *break the signal*, a technique we covered in Lesson 8. So, indicate once for the lane change, switch the indicator off, then indicate again for the slip lane or junction itself.

Slip lanes, then, are used on both motorways and dual-carriageways, but on dual carriageways there are also other types of…

Junctions

There can be roundabouts, which are treated normally, and also minor-road give-way junctions which don't have a slip lane. When turning from the carriageway into a side road, as I said, try to indicate nice-n-early, ideally before braking, and then to slow down for the junction steadily, using your footbrake smoothly, remembering that your brake lights will warn following traffic what you're about to do.

Now, when you're emerging onto the carriageway, turning left, there are two things to remember:

- Your Examiner generally wants both lanes of traffic coming from your right to be clear, not just the lane nearest to you, in case a car in Lane 2 moves into Lane 1 without indicating
- And, also, you need a sufficient gap in traffic before emerging to allow yourself chance to get up to a reasonable speed, before any traffic already on the carriageway catches up with you

But it's turning right, coming from a minor road, cutting across the dual carriageway, that's the trickiest manoeuvre of them all. Believe me, your Examiner could tell you horror stories about learners tackling these junctions on test!

Okay, so picture approaching a dual carriageway from a minor road. If there isn't a central reservation wide enough for you to wait in, then you'll need all of the lanes, from both directions, to be clear before you turn right.

But, if the central reservation's wide enough, then you'll usually be able to cross the two carriageways individually, with a pause in the centre. So it's a bit easier than taking all four lanes in one go, but it's still tricky.

Okay, so let's call the first carriageway that you're going to cross, the one nearest to you, Carriageway A, and the one over on the far side, with traffic coming from your left, Carriageway B.

Now, before crossing Carriageway A, you'll need both lanes from your right to be clear. Then, look to your left, along Carriageway B, because, before you cross Carriageway A you must also be clear of any traffic coming from Carriageway B that's turning right. Now, this is really important. Many drivers seem to think the idea is to just give way to the right – so Carriageway A – then move into the middle, and then give way to the left – Carriageway B. But it isn't. You must look both ways before crossing Carriageway A.

But note, you're only giving way to traffic on Carriageway B that's turning right. At this point, you don't need to worry about guys on Carriageway B who are continuing straight through the junction.

So picture it: you're completely clear from your right, and also clear of any traffic coming from your left that's turning right. Now you can cross Carriageway A.

As you move forward, into the central reservation area, stay fairly straight but with a slight steer over to the right. The aim is to get well into the central reservation, close to the line protecting you from Carriageway B, and then give way to traffic coming from your left.

Now, if you're roughly at right-angles to Carriageway B, three things generally happen:

- Traffic turning right from Carriageway B can still turn right by passing you on your left
- You have an easy view of oncoming traffic through your passenger window
- You don't invite any drivers, who've perhaps followed

you across, to pull-up on your left and block your view
– they're far more likely to end up on your driver's side

Now, you want both lanes from your left to be clear, because from here the plan is to move all the way over to Lane 1 – the left lane, the slow lane, or whatever it is you want to call it – to finish the turn. The plan is not to go into the overtaking lane, unless, that is, the traffic on Carriageway B is at a standstill. In that case, if someone let's you in, then it's okay for you to go into that lane, but then to move across to Lane 1 as soon as possible.

And that's it. Remember, your Examiner's more frightened than you are! Next, in Lesson 14, pack up your picnic bags 'cause we're going for a drive in the country.

LESSON 14:
COUNTRY ROADS

If your local driving test centre's anywhere near nice green countryside then, chances are, your Examiner's going to take you for a nice little drive through some of it, for ten minutes-or-so. Happy days.

Now, in this lesson, I'm essentially going to be talking about three things:

- Speed Limits
- Road positioning
- Overtaking

And, as the list suggests, we'll start with...

Speed Limits

Picture a map of the United Kingdom. England, Scotland, Wales and Northern Ireland. Colour your imaginary map green, to represent all our beautiful green countryside. Now, add to your map grey dots, a dot for each village, town and city in the land, a dot for every place with a name.

Essentially, 99% of roads across the UK fall into one of two speed-limit groups. The green bits on your imaginary map are called *national speed limit* areas, and the grey dots are the residential 30mph limits.

The other 1% of roads have either forty or fifty limits, or are in the 20mph zones that you'll see in some towns and cities. And this 1% is well signposted. Twenty limit zones are marked as you enter the areas, and 40-and-50mph limits also start with a full-sized speed limit sign which are then backed-up by smaller speed limit signs to act as reminders, called repeaters, every few hundred metres-or-so.

The thirty limits, then, are like cosy blankets spread across every village, town and city. So if you can put a name to where you are – London, Edinburgh, Belfast, Cardiff – right down to our smallest, most picture-perfect villages, then chances are, the speed limit will be thirty. And as you enter a town, and pass the thirty sign, then that's it – that sign's all you get – there usually aren't any reminders.

But then, if you turn around and leave the town, on the other side of that thirty sign you'll see, bolted to the same post, a national speed limit sign. That's the white circle with the black diagonal line across it. And you'll see that it doesn't have a number on it. That's because the actual speed limit on a national speed limit road depends on two factors: the type of road, and what you're driving.

In Lesson 13, I described a dual carriageway as having two carriageways, and I said that the speed limit on them is generally the same as on a motorway, 70mph, unless there are signs telling you otherwise. A single carriageway – in other words, a standard country road – has a sixty limit. So, if you drive along an 'A' road up to the point where it changes from a single to a dual carriageway there is also a change of speed limit, from sixty up to seventy. But there aren't any speed limit signs to let you know, it's all about the change of road type.

And the type of vehicle is the other factor on a national speed limit road. Vans, trucks and cars-towing-trailers all have their own speed restrictions. So if a big lorry's holding you up, plodding along at forty in a sixty – well, perhaps it's a sixty limit for you, but not for him. For him it could be a forty.

On test, your Examiner expects you to drive at a *realistic* speed. Essentially that means driving at-or-around the speed limit unless there's a reason for driving more slowly.

Oh, and Examiners like acceleration! Nothing too crazy, but acceleration shows confidence and control. Examiners don't like speeding, though! Speeding's illegal. You might get away with being, say, 10% over the limit for a short period, but don't bank on it. Some Examiners are stricter on this than others.

The majority of drivers, let's say 98%, drive their cars as if they were the carriages of a train, taking their time, merrily following the guy in front. That should be you. So, not one of the 1% creeping around the place, holding everyone else up, or like the other 1%, the dreaded boy racers. No, in driving – if not in life – just follow the crowd.

Anyway, now that we've got you all excited with all this talk of bombing along at sixty, let's calm things down again, and let's make sure that you're in the correct part of the road. Let's talk about...

Road Positioning

We drive on the left. But you're also expected to *keep over to the left*. So, on a nice wide main road, it's not acceptable to be virtually skimming the centre white line. Your general driving position is expected to be about a metre-or-so from the left side of the road, however wide it is. Though, of course, as I've now mentioned many times in previous lessons, the general rule does allow you to move to the right to overtake and to turn right.

When you're driving in lanes, aim to stay in the centre of your lane. That includes slip lanes and those right-turn lanes where you're protected from passing traffic by the hatched road markings.

On narrow country roads, you're expected to be far enough over to the left that when a car comes the other way you don't have to move over to the left to get out of its way. You should already be out of its way. And on country roads, where you're skimming along past hedges, it can be tempting to improve your view around left-hand bends by moving out slightly to the right, towards the middle of the road. But, again, your Examiner expects you to keep well over to the left.

And those hedge-lined left-hand bends are a nightmare. You can't see around them. The thing is, driving, we can usually deal with one problem at a time. So, on a bend, meeting a pedestrian unexpectedly halfway round, we can cope with that, we steer out past. But it's when we meet two problems that we're in trouble. So that pedestrian *plus* a tractor that's coming the other way. Now – if you're going in any way fast at this point – you're in real trouble. I'm afraid those cat-like reactions of yours aren't going to be enough.

So, on country roads, base your speed not only on what you can see, but also on how *far* you can see. And, if you're rounding a bend or cresting a hill – somewhere where you really can't see any further ahead than just a few car lengths – ask yourself: what *can't* I see yet?

But what if you can see something up ahead? What if you're thinking about...

Overtaking

Parked cars on country roads are comparatively rare. So, as discussed way back in Lesson 8, unlike in thirty limits, it's best to indicate before moving out to pass them, especially if there's another car behind you.

Pedestrians, though, unlike parked cars, are actually more common on country roads. After all, there are very few footpaths. And, as I've already said, left-hand bends, especially when they have an overgrown hedge lining the road, are really dangerous in relation to meeting pedestrians – you just don't see them until the last moment.

When you do meet a pedestrian, indicate before pulling out to pass them. Pedestrians ahead of you might be difficult for following drivers to see, so your indicator could be the first warning those following drivers get of the problem up ahead.

And as for the pedestrian himself, walking towards you, what with your car weighing over a ton and doing 50mph... Well, imagine the relief he feels on seeing your indicator flashing away, letting him know that, not only have you seen him, but that you have the situation under control.

On any type of road, town or country, indicate past anything that's moving, including cyclists. So, check your mirrors first, to make sure there isn't some speedy guy already overtaking you, indicate, then give the cyclist plenty of room, a couple of metres at least, as you pass them. Finally, check your mirrors again before pulling back in, just to make sure you haven't left the poor cyclist lying in a heap on the ground!

And you need to do all that without inconveniencing any traffic coming in the other direction. So don't think: *hey, it's only a cyclist* and fire on past. Overtaking anything is serious business and needs serious thought. So don't overtake at junctions or bends or the brows of hills, or outside petrol stations or schools. And if you can't overtake yet, follow the cyclist at a safe distance, a car length-or-two back – close enough that you're ready to overtake when the opportunity comes, but not so close that you'll run into him if he stops. Be patient. It's always the slowest vehicle that dictates the speed of the traffic.

And overtaking cars? Well, on test that's fairly unlikely unless you're on a dual carriageway, which I covered in Lesson 13. So that's something to deal with, with your Supervisor, when the situation arises.

And that's pretty much it for the normal-driving phase of your lessons. We've now covered residential areas, towns, dual car-riageways, and the countryside, and we've discussed the differ-ent types of complex junctions, so traffic lights and round-abouts.

In the next lesson we're going to visit a petrol station.

LESSON 15: PETROL STATIONS

Now that you're – hopefully – getting loads of driving practice, it's time to open your wallet and put some fuel in the car! So, in this lesson we're going to be visiting your local petrol station, to talk about:

- Arriving at the pump
- Petrol or diesel?
- Checking your tyres
- Under the bonnet

Okay, so let's get over to the petrol station and start with...

Arriving At The Pump

So the first thing – even before you head to the petrol station – is do you know how to open your filler cap? Maybe your car has a button somewhere, or maybe you use the ignition key, maybe it has something to do with the central locking... Whatever, find out and practice in the quiet comfort of your own street. If you wait until you're parked at the pump, you might get flustered.

Also, what side is your filler cap on? It's best to park at the pump with your filler cap on the same side as the pump. It is possible to stretch the hose from the fuel pump far enough round to reach across the back of your car, but stretching the hose that far can be a messy business, so it's best avoided, if at all possible.

Oh, and when you do park at the fuel pump, don't get too close. Try to stop with your filler cap at least a metre from the nozzle that you're planning on using.

But which one are you going to use? Is your car...

Petrol Or Diesel

Unless you're driving an electric car, most still take one or the other. So, as you cruise up to the pump, glance over to make sure your type of fuel is available from this pump. Some are only petrol or diesel. Petrol usually has a green handle on the nozzle, diesel black.

It's crucial to make sure you get the correct type of fuel. *Misfuelling*, as it's known, is easily done and expensive to fix. But if you do *misfuel*, and realise your mistake, don't start your engine until the problem has been sorted out – not even to drive away from the pump – because the wrong fuel could easily ruin your engine.

Now, as I said, filling up can be a messy business. The nozzle can leave your hands smelling of fuel, and the hose that unwinds from the pump is often filthy, so don't let it touch your clothes. Also, be careful to watch where you're standing. Diesel is dangerous because it's oily and really slippery, and petrol is highly flammable, so either can ruin your entire day.

Next, check that you get the right amount of fuel. The information screen at the pump will have three figures shown on it. One is the amount of fuel in litres, the second is the pence-per-litre price, and the third figure up there is the total cost of the fuel you've put in so far.

With the nozzle in your tank, begin by squeezing the trigger gently to get the fuel flow started. If you try to start quickly, especially on some older pumps, the trigger might click and the fuel stop. But once you've got the fuel flowing, if you want to fill your tank to the brim, just squeeze the trigger until it clicks – it'll automatically shut off when the tank's full.

However, if you have a certain amount of money you want to spend, or a certain amount of fuel you want to put in, as you get towards that amount, release the trigger. But then gently squeeze the trigger again, slowing things right down, adding just a few pence worth at a time.

Then, when you remove the nozzle, turn it upwards slightly, to avoid drips – otherwise they'll leave nasty streaks down your shiny paintwork.

Oh, and don't smoke. In fact, don't smoke *ever*, but especially while you're filling up! Oh, and don't use your mobile phone while you're filling up, either. I know, I know…you've probably never noticed any sparks flying out from your phone, but it can happen, and the danger from petrol is not from the liquid itself but from its vapour, you can smell it. Anyway, one spark and you're toast!

When you're done, put the nozzle back in the holster, and put your filler cap back on. Then check the price and also your pump's number. That'll speed things up when you come to pay-ing. It's much better to say *Pump 4* than having to point through the attendant's window, vaguely describing your car.

Finally, grab your cash, lock your car, and go and pay.

Now, on your test you'll be asked a couple of *safety questions*. These can be about your car's ancillary controls that we covered in Lesson 7, or they can be about basic car maintenance, the sort of thing you can do at home, or here at the petrol station.

Some of them involve getting under the car's bonnet – and we'll go through those shortly – but let's start with…

Checking Your Tyres

There are two separate things you might be asked about:

- Tyre air pressures
- The condition of your tyres

Let's start with tyre air pressures. Four things:

- Check them early in a journey, when the tyres are still cold
- Know how to find out what the tyre pressures should be
- Find a supply of air and a gauge to check them
- Remove, then replace, the valve dust caps

Now let's add in some detail. As you drive, especially if you drive fast, and especially if you drive on a warm day, your tyres heat up. And, as that happens, so the air inside them expands, which increases the pressure of that air in the tyre. So the recommended tyre pressures for your car are based on cold tyres, tyres that haven't been driven on today for any more than a few miles. So if you have to drive to a petrol station to check your tyre pressures, make it your local one.

The correct air pressure for your tyres can be found online or in your car's handbook. But, to make life easier, most cars also have a sticker on them, with a chart showing the recommended pressures. To find the sticker, start by opening the driver's door and looking along its edge, where the door catch is. If it's not there, try under the bonnet.

On test, you don't need to know the actual tyre pressures for your car, you just need to be able to tell your Examiner where to find them. So, find the tyre pressure chart for your car and take a look at it.

Notice that there's probably a difference in recommended tyre pressures between front and back, and also between when you're driving on your own and when your car's loaded-up with luggage and passengers. There might also be a different pressure shown for motorway driving. And those figures are shown as both PSI – pounds-per-square-inch – and Bar – the metric system. It doesn't matter which one you use.

Then you need to find yourself a tyre pressure gauge and some air. Maybe you have a foot-pump or even a compressor at home, or maybe you need to use the one at the petrol station. That's over where it says *air*, which is usually where your local petrol station also has a water tap that you can use.

Anyway, if you're at the petrol station, park over where it says air. Then see if it's free or coin operated. Then whip off the dust caps from all four tyres and keep them safe. If it's a digital system, set the figure for your car on the machine. Then fit the air valve snugly over your tyre's valve. The machine will make all kinds of hissing noises, then beep when it's finished. Finally, when you're all done, replace the dust caps.

Another question your Examiner might ask is: *how do you check that your tyres are in good condition?* This comes down to two parts of the tyre: the *sidewall* and the *tread.*

The sidewall's the bit that has the writing on it – *Goodyear* or whatever – and you're looking for obvious signs of damage: cuts or bulges around that sidewall. Imagine scraping your hand on a wall and having a sliver of skin that you can lift up, or burning yourself with an iron, giving yourself a blister. That's the kind of thing you're looking for: a cut or a bulge. And damage to the sidewall can't be repaired. The tyre is now dangerous so must be replaced.

Once you've finished with the sidewall, check the tread. The tread's the part of the tyre that actually comes into contact with the road. Those grooves around the tyre must be at least 1.6mm deep. They're there to pump water, from a wet road, away from under your tyre. They're super important.

To check them, you could call into a tyre garage and they'll do it for you. Or you can do it yourself, either with a tread depth gauge, or by running your fingernail around inside one of the grooves, feeling for the bumps that are positioned every few inches in there. Those things are called *wear bars*, and they're roughly 1.6mm up from the bottom of the groove. So, as the rubber wears down, the wear bars kind of come up, until, when they reach the top of the groove, flush with main part of tyre itself, that tyre's worn out.

So, that's the tyres looked over. Now let's check...

Under The Bonnet

Get your Supervisor to show you how to open the bonnet on your car. Again, on test, your Examiner might ask you to tell him how you check something that's under there, but he won't ask you to actually do it, so you won't be getting your hands dirty – you're not expected to be mechanic, just to pass a driving test!

Anyway, grab a rag or a cloth and have a quick look around the engine. The Examiner might ask you to explain how to check and refill any one of the fluids under there. So that's:

- Oil
- Coolant
- Brake fluid
- Windscreen washers

And some cars also have power steering fluid under there as well. Get your Supervisor to run through each of them: how to check them, and if necessary, how to top them up. Use your cloth to wipe things clean, and to protect your hands – especially when you're refilling the coolant. If the engine's been running, it's hot in there and the coolant could potentially be boiling.

Okay, so now you've proved yourself on your local petrol station's forecourt – and so prepared yourself for the safety questions you'll be asked on test – it's time to move on to the last few lessons. You've a few exercises – or manoeuvres – that you'll have to do on test, so we'll crack-on with those now, and start, in Lesson 16, with the emergency stop.

LESSON 16:
EMERGENCY STOP

At some point during your test, your Examiner will get you to pull over at the side of the road. Then, when you've stopped, he'll say: 'Shortly I'm going to ask you to stop as though in an emergency, as though a child has run out onto the road in front of you. When I give you the signal, I want you to stop the car quickly but under control.'

The signal, by the way, is him raising his right hand and saying: *Stop!*

Now, before you move away, make sure that you're completely clear in your mirrors. If there's anything following you, your Examiner won't ask you to do the emergency stop. Instead, he'll probably just get you to pull over again, to let any traffic pass by, before trying it all over again.

So, nice clear mirrors and move away. Then drive *normally*. I know that sounds obvious but some people either drive really slowly – as though that's going to give them some kind of advantage – or else they take off like a rally driver, on a wave of emergency-stop-fuelled adrenaline.

So, accelerate and change up normally. And deal with any problems that might arise normally, too. You're not going to be asked to do this halfway past a bin lorry or a school bus. So, as I said, slow down and deal with any problems normally.

Anyway, once you're finally on the move, your Examiner will

prepare to give you the signal. You'll be in 2nd or 3rd gear – or maybe the signal will come during the actual gear change – and you'll be doing around 20-to-30mph. He'll check that there's nothing behind you, and that you're not going to cause any problems for anybody up ahead of you, either. Then he'll give you the signal...*Stop!*

Now your Examiner wants to see six things:

- A fast reaction time
- Quick, progressive braking
- Footbrake then clutch
- Hands on the wheel until you've stopped
- Secure the car
- Full observation before moving away again

Let's add in some detail. When you're given the signal, you're expected to move your foot immediately to the brake – a child has run out – so you don't need to check your mirrors first!

Then brake *progressively*. Try saying to yourself *push* as you brake. Or try counting out *one, two, three* as you increase the pressure on the brake pedal. What you're looking for is a way of preventing yourself from just stamping down on the pedal.

So, yes, you're trying to stop the car quickly – ideally within a couple of car lengths – without needing the car's Antilock Braking System, its ABS, to help you control it, but the level of braking needed – the urgency – will be something like you've been caught out by a traffic light changing to red. Nothing too crazy!

When you practice, start fairly gently, increasing your pressure on the brakes as your confidence grows. When the brakes are on, get the clutch down, all the while keeping your hands up on the wheel. So it's brakes *then* clutch. Preferably not both together. And definitely not clutch first.

Now, when the car's stopped, put the handbrake on and change into neutral. Then, when your Examiner tells you to move away again, say to yourself: *three, two, one*. That's:

- Three: All three mirrors
- Two: Both blind spots
- One: Back to the rear-view mirror

Try not to leave any of those safety checks out. Then, if you can move away again safely, do so. But if there's a car coming up behind you, and you don't think you can move away safely before it reaches you, just wait. Don't indicate. Don't move. Just wait. See what the other guy does. If he sits behind you, indicate right and move away again. If he drives past, let him go, then you drive away.

Now, let's rewind a bit. After you've stopped the car, and you have it secured, your Examiner will say, 'I won't ask you to do that again. Move on when you're ready.'

Now, what he's doing here is *covering* himself. He's telling you that you're *not* going to be asked to do another emergency stop. So if, say, later on in the test, the Examiner's brother comes driving along towards you and, out of habit, your Examiner waves at him to say *hello*; but *you* mistakenly think he's telling you to do another emergency stop. So you hit the brakes! Well, you can just imagine the potential carnage that miscommunication could cause!

And that's it. *Easy-peasy*. The entire thing, start-to-finish, takes less than a minute. Your Examiner here is just seeing what you do when you're put under pressure – checking your reaction – then seeing how well you control the brakes. Then, finally, he's watching your safety checks before you move away again.

Practice on dry roads and wet roads. Practice in both 2nd and 3rd gears. Practice when changing from 2nd to 3rd. And practice over a range of speeds.

LESSON 17: REVERSING MANOEUVRES

First of all, you're not alone... This is the lesson everybody dreads! As I'm sure you know, on your test you'll be asked to carry out an exercise that involves reversing. It'll only take you two-or-three minutes to complete, yet the reversing manoeuvre is responsible for a quarter of all test fails, so it's really important to get loads of practice to make sure you don't fall into that statistic.

We're going to be talking about six different manoeuvres in this lesson, but not all of them are required for your test. I'll explain why in a moment, but first the list of manoeuvres:

- The turn in the road
- Reversing around a corner
- Reversing into a parking bay
- Parallel parking
- Pulling over on the right and reversing
- Driving forwards into a parking bay and reversing back out again

Now, the official driving test syllabus recommends you practice all six manoeuvres, so how come you only need to be really good at four of them? Well, two words: *Northern Ireland.* Tests in Northern Ireland still do *the turn in the road* and *reverse around a corner* exercises, but the rest of the UK has dropped those two in favour of *pulling over on the right and reversing* and *driving forwards into a parking bay and reversing back out again.*

So, whether you're doing your test in Great Britain or Northern Ireland, your Examiner only has four manoeuvres to choose from. But, as I said, it's recommended you practice all six as they're all skills that'll come in handy for real-world driving.

But, wherever you're doing your test, and whatever manoeuvre your Examiner chooses for you, all the manoeuvres have three things in common, three things your Examiner will be watching for:

- Control
- Accuracy
- Observation

Let's start with control. Your Examiner wants to see you keeping your car nice-n-slow, using the clutch smoothly. He wants to see you steering nice-n-quickly, but avoiding *dry steering* as much as possible. That means not turning the steering-wheel while the car's stationary. He wants to see that you stop smoothly, and that you use the handbrake where necessary.

And he wants you to manoeuvre accurately. If he asks you to reverse into a parking bay he expects you to finish with all four wheels between the lines. But you don't have to be perfect. Maybe you end up nearer one line than the other, or maybe you end up a bit wonky. No matter, provided you're in the bay, it's fine.

And you don't necessarily need to get neatly into the parking bay first go. On any manoeuvre, you're allowed to reverse twice if you need to. So, if you mess up on the reverse into the bay, you can always pull forward to straighten up, then reverse back in again.

And if you touch a kerb, don't panic! Yes, you've made a mistake. Yes, your Examiner has noticed. So, yes, he'll mark your mistake as a fault. But, no, it'll not necessarily be a serious fault. So, no, it'll not necessarily be a fail.

Now, having said that, if you do manage to thump into a kerb, then, yes, unfortunately it may well be a fail. But, even then, hopefully you'll still be given the benefit of the doubt. And anyway, the last thing you want to do on test is to give up. So, if you do touch a kerb, try not to worry. Just finish the manoeuvre, finish the test, and keep your fingers crossed!

And your Examiner wants you to be observant. Very observant. The *observation* aspect of your manoeuvre is the *safety* aspect of your manoeuvre, and the driving test is all about safety. So, before you start your manoeuvre, look around for other traffic and for pedestrians. Check all three mirrors and both blind spots. Wait until everything's clear before you begin.

Then, during the manoeuvre, try to be constantly aware of what's going on around you. If other traffic turns up, do the opposite to them. So if they wait, you can continue, but if they move, then you must stay still until they've gone.

As you reverse, look where you're going as much as possible. Look through the back window as well as using your rear-view mirror and side mirrors. And keep checking those blind spots.

If your car has one, you can use a reversing camera, but you must also look around for yourself, not just rely on what's on the screen.

So, to recap, during your reversing manoeuvre your Examiner watches your control, accuracy and observation. But what he *doesn't* do is set a stop watch. Within reason, it doesn't matter how long the manoeuvre takes you to do. In fact, if you do manoeuvre quickly then you're almost certainly not being observant enough to keep your Examiner happy. Take your time. There's no rush.

And, as I'll keep on saying, get loads of practice. Honestly, it's not unusual for new drivers to need to do each manoeuvre twenty-or-thirty times before they're getting the hang of them. And

that's with a professional instructor. So, if it's just you and your Supervisor working together, be super patient with each other!

Oh, and look-up the manoeuvres online. You'll find loads of videos and other content available for each of them.

Anyway, we've talked about manoeuvring in general, so now let's briefly discuss each of the manoeuvres in turn. Remember, though, that although it's recommended that you practice all six of the manoeuvres, you'll only be asked to do one of them on test. And also remember that there are only four of the six manoeuvres that *your* Examiner can choose from, depending on where in the Country you're taking your test. I'll remind you again, as we go through them, which of them you might be asked to do.

Let's start, then, with what is probably the most basic of the manoeuvres – so the foundation on which the other manoeuvres are built – and one that's well worth practising, although, nowadays, it's only tested in Northern Ireland. It's the one we all know as the *three point turn*, though it's correct title is the...

Turn In The Road

This manoeuvre starts with you pulled over on the side of the road. Then your Examiner says: 'I'd like you to turn the car around in the road to face the opposite direction. Try not to touch the kerbs.'

Note that your Examiner doesn't call this a three-point-turn because, as I've said, if necessary, you're allowed to reverse more than once. So it's okay for this manoeuvre to become a *five-point-turn*.

Drive slow but steer fast. The idea is to keep the car moving really slowly, at a walking pace, using clutch control – so easing the clutch up to just over the biting point, then squeezing it down to just below the biting point – while steering quickly to full lock, heading over to the far kerb. Then, as you arrive at the kerb, straighten the steering and stop. Try to stop about a foot from the kerb.

All the manoeuvres are made easier by finding reference points that you can use to help you with your accuracy. The reference point here, to help you judge your distance from the kerb, is to line-up the kerb – that's the one that you can now see underneath your door mirror – with your door, so maybe stopping with the kerb just above the buttons that control your windows, for example.

When you're first practising this, get your Supervisor to find you an area with low kerbs, so that when you're getting the hang of this it doesn't matter if you touch the kerb.

For the reverse leg, same idea, steer quickly to full-left-lock while keeping the car moving slowly. Then steer back to the right and stop just before you bump the kerb. Your reference point, looking down at the kerb over your right shoulder, will probably be something like lining up the kerb with the bottom corner of the door window.

On the third – and hopefully, final – leg, pull forward, steering to full-right-lock, and holding the steering on until you're clear of the kerb. Then straighten-up and drive away.

So there are three distinct parts to the manoeuvre, but essentially all three are the same:

- Look all around for traffic and pedestrians
- Stay slow

- Steer quickly to full lock, heading for the far kerb
- Straighten up
- Stop just before you touch the kerb
- Handbrake on

The next manoeuvre we'll look at is also only tested in Northern Ireland, but is also well-worth us all practising. It's…

Reversing Around A Corner

To begin, your Examiner asks you to pull over just before you reach a side road on your left. He then points to the side road and says: 'This is the road I want you to reverse into. I'd like you to…'

- Drive just past the road and stop
- Then reverse in, keeping reasonably close to the kerb
- And go back for some distance into the new road and stop

So, you start by driving forwards, across the face of the road you'll be reversing into. As you pass, have a quick look into it, to make sure it's safe for you to reverse into. You're looking for road-works, children playing, parked cars blocking your way, that kind of thing. Now, if you think it's not safe, discuss why with your Examiner, who will then tell you whether or not he agrees with you, and whether or not you should continue with the manoeuvre. But if he doesn't agree with you – don't worry – you're not marked down as having made a mistake in any way.

Continue for a car-length-or-two past the corner and stop, a couple of feet from the kerb, to give yourself plenty of room. Select reverse, look all around – you know the drill, all three mirrors, both blind spots – then reverse slowly, looking out through the rear window as much as possible, back to the point where your rear wheel reaches the beginning of the corner. Then stop.

Now, this point, when your rear wheel's at the start of the corner, is your *turning point*. It's the point where you're going to begin steering around the corner, and here you need a reference point. Maybe you can best find your reference point by using your passenger-side door-mirror. Or maybe you can see the kerb in your passenger-side back-seat window. Ideally you're going to use a combination of both. Anyway, play around with it until you find what works best for you. Maybe even get your Supervisor to look out at the back wheel for you, to tell you when it lines up with the start of the corner.

Then, stationary at your turning point, look all around again, including into the side road, and wait for any traffic or pedestrians to pass by.

All clear? Okay, turn the steering into the corner, turning the wheel the way you want the back of the car to go. Start with one full turn of the wheel, and see if that works, see if that has you roughly following the kerb. Maybe three-quarters of a turn might work better for you. But whatever you use, be warned that pretty-much every corner you meet has a slightly different shape to it, so is slightly different as you reverse around it.

Now, as you come into the new road you'll see the kerb again, both in your door mirror and in your back window. Then, if say you've got three-quarters of a turn of steering on, you've got three quarters to take off. But not all at once. You take that steering off a quarter turn at a time, counting those quarters, taking off the final quarter just as you come parallel with the new kerb.

Then just run back another couple of car lengths and stop. Go back far enough that if someone came up behind you, they'd have enough room to nip past and get back into their own half of the road before they reached the give way line.

Job done. What about...

Reversing Into A Parking Bay

Remember, the two manoeuvres we've just discussed are now-adays only used on tests in Northern Ireland. But this one, *reversing into a parking bay*, and the next one, *parallel parking*, are used on test everywhere. So you all need to pay particular attention to these two!

Anyway, reversing into a parking bay is done at your local test centre, either at the beginning or end of your test, and into a bay either on your left or right.

Whichever way you're going – so left or right – start by moving forward, your car about a metre away from the end of the bay, then stop with your shoulder lined-up with the first line of the bay you've chosen – let's call it Line 1. Look all around. If necessary, wait for people to pass by. Then, moving forward slowly, steer one turn of the wheel away from the bay.

The second line of the bay you've chosen, funnily enough, we'll call Line 2. Now, as Line 2 passes your shoulder, straighten up – so take that one turn back off – then continue forward until Line 2 is at your reference point, then stop.

The reference point here will depend on whether you're reversing into a bay on your right or left, so practice both. For a bay on your left, it'll be lining-up Line 2 with the bottom corner of your passenger-side back-seat window. And for a bay on your right, it'll be down along the side of your driver's door-window.

Look all around again. Then reverse, very slowly, steering full-lock, into the bay. Straighten up again as you see Line 2 in your door mirror.

Once you're in the bay – very important, this – pause and look all around again. Check all three mirrors and both blind spots before running back fully into the bay.

Now, once you're safe-n-sound in the bay, if you want, you can open your door and take a look at the white line outside, to check

your position in the bay. Remember that, as long as you're between the lines, that's good enough, even if you're much closer
to one line than the other. It's only if you're on or over a line
that you'll need to pull forward a car length-or-two, steering as
necessary to get yourself between the lines, and reverse back in
again.

Stay slow, stay observant – especially for pedestrians – and take
your time. Next, then, is another manoeuvre that you could be
asked to do anywhere in the UK. It's…

Parallel Parking

On test, your Examiner asks you to pull over at the side of the
road, then points to a car parked in front of you, and says: 'Pull
up alongside the car in front of us. Then use reverse gear to park
close to and parallel with the kerb. Then stop, roughly within
two car lengths of the car.'

So, from your start position, make sure you're clear all around –
nothing coming from front or back – and pull out from the kerb
to move up alongside the car. You're aiming to be about a metre
away from it, parallel with it, with your wheels straight. Then
try to stop so that the back of your car is a metre-or-so past the
car you're using. That takes some judgement, as different types
of cars are different lengths.

When you stop, indicate left, keep your footbrake on and select
reverse gear. So now you've got your indicator flashing away,
your brake lights on, and your white reversing light on. So the
back of your car's lit up like a Christmas tree!

Now, look all around. Wait for any traffic that's passing and for
pedestrians crossing behind you, or walking close to you on the
footpath. All clear? Okay, you're ready to start reversing.

Reverse slowly, steering one full turn of the wheel towards the kerb. After about a car length, when you're pointing diagonally across the road, aiming at the kerb, angled in at about forty-five degrees, straighten up.

Then keep the car still and look all around. Be especially careful of cars approaching from behind you, as they'll be in your blind spot, over your right shoulder.

Next, you're going back another car length-or-so to your reference point for this manoeuvre. Find your reference point by looking in your door mirror as you approach the kerb. Notice how the amount of tarmac you can see in the mirror is shrinking. Watch the kerb, and it's relation to, say, your door handle. Take note of your reference point. Then look all around again.

By stopping at this point, two things happen. First: your reference point will always be more accurate than if you try to find it on the move. And, second: by stopping you ensure that you have plenty of time to look all around – so you don't need to rush, or worse, forget, to do your all-round observation again, at this point.

All clear? Okay, so moving slowly again, steer quickly to full-right-lock. At this point, your car's virtually pivoting around on your driver's-side rear-wheel, swinging into the parking space. And let it swing in, until you're parallel with the kerb, then stop.

How far from the kerb are you? Miles away? Next time, get a little closer – and revise your reference point – before going to full-right-lock. Touching the kerb? Next time, stop a little earlier, so you can see a bit more tarmac in the mirror, before steering to full-right-lock.

Try this technique a couple of times. It won't take long for you to be able to consistently find an accurate reference point. You could even practice this in a deserted car park. Just reverse towards a kerb, at forty-five degrees, and work-out your reference point in the door mirror. Three-or-four goes, and you'll be swinging it in there perfectly!

Now, once you've got the reference point worked out, as you swing into the kerb, take some of the steering off, just before parallel, so just before you stop. Your Examiner asked you to finish *close to, and parallel with* the kerb, but note that he didn't say that you must have the wheels completely straight. So, when you're parallel with the kerb, you're finished. Secure the car. Your work here is done.

Okay. Four down, two to go. Next…

Pulling Over On The Right Then Reversing For Two Car Lengths

This one's not used on test in Northern Ireland, this one's for Great Britain only.

So, there you are, on test, driving down a residential street, when your Examiner asks you to, 'Pull over on the right-hand side of the road, when it's safe to do so.'

Back to basics. Don't park blocking bus-stops or driveways, don't stop close to junctions, including opposite them. And don't stop close to a parked car, it's only going to make it tricky to see past it – in a minute-or-two – when you're asked to move away again.

Anyway, choose your spot, and then prepare as if you're turning right. So, mirrors, indicators, position in the road, then give way to oncoming traffic before moving across to the right-hand kerb. Line the kerb up in your windscreen, maybe six inches-or-so in from the right-hand edge of it, then straighten your steering, stop, and secure the car.

Now your Examiner says: 'Now reverse for two car lengths, keeping reasonably close to the kerb.'

So, into reverse, look all about, including forwards, then reverse slowly. You're trying to keep parallel with the kerb, around a foot-or-so away from it. You can use the door mirror to help you gauge your distance from the kerb, but try to look back, through the rear window, as much as possible. Find a point on the lower edge of your back window where the kerb lines up, then, if you need to adjust your steering, only use small amounts, no more than a quarter turn of the wheel at a time, and remember that, if things go pear-shaped, you can always pull forward a touch, straighten up, and reverse again.

Now, if you find it tricky to reverse in a straight line, it could be because you're thinking in terms of turning right or left. So, instead, think of turning the wheel either *towards* or *away from* the kerb. Try putting your hands at the twelve o'clock position on the wheel, then moving them slightly towards the kerb. Towards and away from the kerb are the same whether you're driving backwards or forwards.

Throughout this straight reverse, try to keep your observation going. Look back, to watch for pedestrians and guys driving out of their driveways, and also look forwards, and wait if any oncoming traffic that passes by. After a couple of car lengths, stop again. As usual, try not to block any driveways or bus-stops.

Finally, your Examiner will simply tell you to move away when you're ready.

This is tricky because you have to give way to oncoming traffic as well as those coming up behind you, and you're going to have to drive all the way across from the right to the left-hand side of the road. So you'll need nice big gaps in traffic from both directions before you indicate left and check the left blind-spot – one last time – before moving away.

Oh, and if during the time it takes you to do this manoeuvre another car turns up and parks in front of you, making it difficult for you to take safe observation before moving away, then your Examiner will step in to assist you, and give you updates on any oncoming traffic.

Okay! Nearly there. Last one! And again, this one isn't done in Northern Ireland. This one is…

Driving Forwards Into A Parking Bay Then Reversing Back Out

…and it's done in a local car park. So, as you enter the car park, watch for direction signs and arrows, speed limit signs and, of course, pedestrians.

Your Examiner will ask you to select a bay – it could be on your right or left – and to drive forwards into it and park.

So, use your mirrors, indicate, and check your blind-spot before you start your turn into the bay.

Your reference point for steering will be in the respective side window of the side you're driving into. Again, practice to find a spot in the side window that works for you. The idea is to reach your reference point, then to steer in with full-lock, straightening up as you enter the bay.

Like the other manoeuvres, if you don't manage to steer accurately into the bay on the first attempt, you can reverse back out a car length-or-so, and try again.

Anyway, once you're in the bay, with the car secure, your Examiner will ask you to reverse back out of the space and drive away.

The danger here is in the front of your car swinging round and potentially hitting the car parked alongside you if you steer too soon. So, as you reverse, stay perfectly straight for around three-quarters of the length of your car, before steering round, all the while being aware of what the front of your car's doing.

LESSON 18: WHAT TO EXPECT ON TEST DAY

Lots of folk, after failing a driving test, will say, *oh well, at least I know what to expect next time.* Nobody likes nasty surprises. That's why schools focus so much on past exam papers and exam technique. Now, when it comes to your driving test, I'm sure you'll not be too surprised to hear that the better you are at driving the higher your chance of success! But, having said that, knowing what to expect is a big thing. So, in this lesson, we're going to focus on preparation for the test that goes beyond the actual driving.

So, first off we'll look at the importance of visiting your local test centre, getting a feel for both the place and also for what goes on there. Then we'll run through:

- Booking your test
- In the test centre
- Your car
- The eyesight test
- The safety questions
- Your Examiner
- The marking system
- Abandoned tests
- Test route directions
- Independent driving
- The result

But, before we crack on with those, as promised, first a quick word about the importance of visiting the driving test centre beforehand…

The centre you'll be using might not be exactly what you'd call *local*. It might be miles away. But gaining the experience of driving into the place and parking, of walking over to the waiting area, of watching a test candidate walking over to his car with his Examiner, watching him doing his eyesight test and his safety question, then watching him drive away… All that stuff's pure gold when it comes to your test preparation.

You can check driving test start times online, so as to time your visit to the test centre for you to watch an actual test getting underway. Then, when that test has gone, take a look at the layout of the road system there, the speed limit and the road arrows.

Also, get a feel for the roads and junctions around the test centre. Look at it on a road map. How many ways in and out of the immediate area are there? Chances are, driving test routes will take in all of those roads and junctions, so spend as much time as possible driving around, getting to know the area.

And test routes, too. Within the local area you're bound to find somewhere with a bunch of driving school cars working on junctions or manoeuvres. They're there because their pupils get taken there on test. So, again, take a look around.

Okay, so, back to our list for this lesson. And let's start by talking about…

Booking Your Test

Now, not wanting to state the obvious here, but only book your test when you can drive safely, without any more than the occasional word of advice from your Supervisor. If you're still being reminded to change gear or to brake, or who has priority at a junction, then you need much more driving practice.

There's no secret here: the more you drive the better you get. So practice as much as you can and continue to revise these lessons. Oh, and also re-read the *Highway Code*. You see, things that you once only thought of as theory will make much more sense now that you're thinking of your practical driving test. Your theory was like reading the handbook on a sport you've never played. Now you're in the game.

Book the test online at the official website. The official website doesn't charge a booking fee. The rip-off sites do. Book a test that's at least a month away, to give yourself plenty of time for the all-important mock tests and final revision. And book your test for a sensible time. I mean, do you really want to be adding to the stress of doing your test by doing it in the middle of the school run? Hopefully you're only ever going to take one driving test in your life, so why worry if you have to wait another week-or-two for a good time to do it?

So, now that you've taken a run up to your local test centre, and you've also got the test booked, let's talk about what happens on test day...

In The Test Centre

Well, on your test day, don't be late! But don't be too early, either. About fifteen minutes before your test appointment is perfect, not half-an-hour – you'll just be sitting there, getting more-n-more nervous.

Get your paperwork ready for your Examiner to...er...examine. He'll want to see your provisional licence and your theory test pass letter. And also your passport, if your licence doesn't in-clude photographic ID. If you can't find any of your documents leading up to your test, go online or phone the test centre for advice.

So, when you meet your Examiner he'll check your driving documents. He'll also ask you to sign a declaration to confirm that your car's legal for you to drive. Then he'll ask you if you'd like your Supervisor or Instructor to accompany you on the test, to sit in the back of the car. Discuss with your Supervisor or Instructor what your answer's going to be in advance.

The advantage of someone going with you is that, especially if you fail, whoever's accompanied you will have seen first-hand the mistakes you made. The disadvantage is that you might feel under even more pressure, what with two people watching your every move. It's up to you.

Anyway, formalities completed, Examiner smiling, butterflies turning somersaults in your stomach, you finally head out to the car park to start the test. Now, on test, for the price of your fee, the test centre has supplied you with a Driving Examiner, but not with a car. Small detail, I know, but you have to supply one of those yourself! So let's make sure you're organised, let's talk about...

Your Car

Though, hopefully, it'll be either your Supervisor or Instructor who'll take care of this for you. But, just in case...

So, your car needs to be legal, obviously. Taxed, insured, MoT'd. And, if you have them, you might as well take all the documents with you, in case there's a query about anything.

And your car needs to be roadworthy. Just waving an MoT certificate around won't impress anyone if your exhaust's clearly hanging off! And your car needs four good tyres. And head restraints. And 'L' plates – set so that they don't block the Examiner's view. And, yes, he will check all this stuff.

Same goes for the lights. If your Examiner notices that one's not working your test won't go ahead. Warning lights, too. If the dashboard's telling him that the car has a problem, then he won't take you out on test.

You also need a mirror, fixed to the windscreen, for your Examiner's use. One of those suction-cup ones will do. They cost about a fiver. The Examiner does provide a sat-nav, though, so you don't need one of those. Oh, and if there's one already in your car, turn it off for the test. Your mobile phone, too.

Finally, give your pride-n-joy a clean. Clean cars drive better, everyone knows that. And a freshly washed-n-vacuumed car, with nice clean windows, will give your Examiner a positive impression of you and your preparation.

Now, if there is a problem with your car, and, for whatever reason, your Examiner refuses to take you out on test, I'm afraid you lose your fee and you have to re-book. So make sure you've done your homework, and everything's sorted.

In the test centre, hopefully you've parked neatly in a parking space. Most test centres have spaces reserved for driving test candidates, so go and take a look at them. On test day, make sure it's easy for you drive away from the space at the start of the test. So, if necessary, reverse in.

Finally, remember that your test will usually be at the same time as other test candidates, so the centre could be busy with those other candidates arriving at the same time as you. And also try not to get in the way of guys returning from tests. There's often only a few minutes between one test ending and another starting, so keep out of the way, especially of cars doing reverse parking manoeuvres.

Okay, now things are getting serious. Picture yourself heading over to your car with your Examiner, when he stops, and asks you to stand next to him, before telling you that you're going to start with an...

Eyesight Test

You're asked to read a car's number-plate from twenty-odd metres away. No problem? Great. Yes problem? Then your Examiner heads back into the test centre for his tape measure. Yes...seriously. Then he measures an exact twenty metres away from a car, and gets you to try again. And if you still can't read it then I'm afraid you've just failed your entire driving test.

Oh, and yes, if you wear contacts or glasses then you can do the eyesight test with those in-or-on, but then you must do the rest of the test with them too.

Once that's done, it's over to the car and the first of the...

Safety Questions

You'll be asked two questions in total, one now and one when you're actually driving. The driving question will be something like demonstrating how the windscreen washers-n-wipers work. But at the test centre, before the drive, your Examiner will perhaps ask you to explain one of the procedures that we covered at the petrol station in Lesson 15. So, perhaps something like how to check the oil level, or perhaps to talk him through the procedure for checking tyre pressures.

Now, if you've been through all the lessons on here, you'll have covered everything you need to know in regard to the safety questions. But if you want more information, there are loads of videos online, covering all the questions in detail.

So what happens next? Who is this guy standing before you, wearing a fluorescent vest and clutching a leather folder? Good question. So, let's talk about...

Your Driving Examiner

Well, his work schedule for the day allows for about an hour for each test, but that includes the five minutes the two of you have already spent meeting in the test centre and now out in the car park. Then you'll spend around forty minutes on the actual drive, then another five minutes-or-so back in the car park, after the drive, when your Examiner will discuss your test drive with you and, hopefully, organise your shiny new driving licence.

After that, he wishes you well, dashes back to his office – super quick – for a coffee, then he heads back round to the waiting room for his next victim. Sorry, not victim, *test candidate...*

So, after all your hours-upon-hours of preparation, and your miles-upon-miles of driving, it all comes down to the next forty minutes. Now, everybody who was thoroughly prepared – and I mean everybody – tells me their test flew by. In fact, strange as it may sound to you now, lots of people tell me that they ended up actually enjoying their driving test! It's that feeling: the day is finally here, so pre-test nerves are fading, adrenaline is kicking in. You're confident as a driver, you've practised your manoeuvres until you're doing them in your sleep, you're familiar with your car and your surroundings, you've realised that your Examiner's actually a really nice bloke, and it's slowly dawning on you that you're going to get through this, that you're actually going to pass.

But if, on the other hand, you're not truly ready for it, it could turn into a very long forty minutes indeed. Because, although, yes, your Examiner is a really nice bloke, he's not your Supervisor, so he's not there to help you out. No, his job is to direct you around the test route and to mark down any mistakes that you might make.

Now, if you get into difficulties, he's not just going to passively sit there and let you crash – he will intervene if necessary – but if it is necessary for him to intervene, so if you do need help to drive safely, then that will be a test fail. The idea is for you to be able to drive safely and legally around the test route on your own. No help required.

So unlike, say, a history essay, there are no 'B' or 'C' grades on a driving test. It's either 'A' or 'F'. That's it. Pass or fail.

Having said that, remember that your Examiner only marks the mistakes you make, the faults. He doesn't officially note down the good stuff during your drive, the things that you do well.

Ah…but even though he doesn't officially note what you do well, he is human, and as I've said, first impressions can go a long way. And so too does the impression that you're well prepared in your actual driving for the test. So, a candidate who's driven well, right up to the point where they – *oh no* – make a mistake, is more likely to be given the benefit of the doubt than one who's looked a bit dodgy from the very beginning.

Examiners are referees. They're trained to follow a rule book. But they're not machines. They have opinions, they make judgements.

And take no notice of all the stuff you hear about Examiners having quotas, or being more inclined to pass people on a Monday morning, or whatever. It's all nonsense. Just make sure you're well prepared, drive to make a good impression, and you'll sail through. Even if there's going to be a full moon that night!

So the test is negatively marked. Which, if you think about it, means that as far as your Examiner's concerned, you begin the test with a pass. Which means that *your job is simply to make sure that you don't fail.*

So…wait. Hang on. You start the driving test with a pass? Yep. You sure do. Your Examiner – and the whole-entire Government, for that matter – *want* you to pass.

Sounds crazy? Maybe, but see, drivers are the ultimate tax payers. When you have a car, you'll pay tax on your car and its insurance, you'll pay tax on its spares and repairs, and a huge amount of tax on its fuel. You'll pay tax just to be allowed to use the road. What, you think you own your car just because you buy it with your hard-earned money? No, you will be the keeper of that car. I mean, just try leaving an untaxed car parked out on the street to see who really owns it! You'll be waving bye-bye to your pride-n-joy as you watch it being towed away!

So, the system (here at least) is on your side. Most adults drive. But not everybody passes first time. The pass-rate is around fifty percent. So, for every eight candidates, four pass, four fail.

Now, of the four who fail, one either isn't yet ready for the test, or just makes a huge one-off mistake. Happens to the best of us. But the other three failures, statistically:

- One fails in relation to priority
- One fails because they aren't using their mirrors correctly or checking those blind spots
- One fails during their manoeuvre, usually in relation to observation

So, folks, don't make it easy for your Examiner to fail you. Get back to basics, and get those basics right:

- Moving away procedure
- Junctions and priority
- Mirrors and blind spots
- Manoeuvres

Okay, so we've talked about the way the test is negatively marked, the way your Examiner only marks down your faults, not what you do well. Now let's talk in a bit more detail about…

The Marking System

There are three levels of fault that your Examiner can mark against you on test. The most serious is a *dangerous* fault. That's one where your Examiner actually takes action to avoid either an accident or a potentially dangerous situation. He can take action verbally or physically – so taking control of the car by perhaps steering or using the handbrake – or if the car has dual controls, by having to use those.

Dangerous faults are a fail. You're not allowed any of those.

Next down on the scale are *serious* faults. Just one serious fault is also a test fail. So, as far as we're concerned, both dangerous and serious faults are essentially the same thing. You're not allowed to score any of either of them.

Finally, there are *driving* faults. These used to be known, back-in-the-day, as *minor* faults. So, slight mistakes. Maybe you forgot to check your mirror back there before indicating, or maybe your blind spot check before moving away on your hill-start was a bit too casual for your Examiner's liking. Whatever, these are the kind of things that are scored against you as driving faults.

At the end of the test, the driving faults are added up. Now, you're allowed up to fifteen of them, so if you end up with sixteen-or-more, even if you don't have any dangerous or serious faults, it's a fail. But to score sixteen faults you'd have to be getting a driving fault, so making a noticeable mistake, every two-and-a-half minutes, which probably means you're not yet ready to drive on your own anyway!

But there is another way you can fail the test through your driving faults, and that's if you keep making the same mistake. So, no, stalling the engine isn't necessarily a serious fault, provided you make the car safe before re-starting. But if you *keep on* stalling…three…four times, then your Examiner's likely to decide you need more practice, so he's likely to upgrade those driving faults into a serious fault.

So, to recap. There are four ways you can fail the test:

- One-or- more dangerous fault
- One-or-more serious fault
- Sixteen-or-more driving faults
- Or a pattern of committing the same driving fault

So, you could reach the end of your test, back in the test centre car park, and be told that your driving hasn't reached the required standard, that you've failed. But what about if you don't even make it back to the test centre, what about…

Abandoned Tests

Well, in a really extreme situation, either you or your Examiner could decide to call the test off mid-way through, to *abandon* it. It's rare but it does happen. Maybe your brain has just had a meltdown and you've jumped a red light. You've never done it before, but there you are, these things happen. So you tell your Examiner that you're aware of your mistake and you no longer want to continue with the test.

Your Examiner replies that it's up to you, that he completely understands, and then directs you to pull over at the side of the road. Once you're safe and secure, he asks you to turn off the engine. Then he talks to you briefly about the drive, maybe even gives you a couple of positives to take away from the experience. But then he gets out and leaves you! So, no, he doesn't drive you back to the test centre. Wherever you end up stopping, that's where you're left. Nightmare. Now you need to phone your Supervisor and have him come out to collect both you and the car. And that could take ages.

So unless, as I said, it's a *really* extreme situation, don't give up.

Guys that give up are left demoralised and deflated. They might even question whether or not this driving lark is really for them.

But if, on the other hand, after making a horrendous mistake, you just pull on your big-boy pants and finish the test then you'll gain the experience of having driven a proper driving test route with a proper Driving Examiner, who will give you proper feedback on the entire drive. So, even though you've failed, you've had your money's worth, and your confidence will have survived the ordeal.

So reaching the point where you can drive round a test route with an Examiner is a huge step along the way to becoming a good driver. But not everyone passes, not first-time, anyway. Some need two-or-three goes. But it's not the end of the world; everyone gets there eventually. And the experience and the confidence you'll gain from completing a test – even if you don't pass – means you'll be right back in there, even more determined to pass next time.

Don't give up.

And that includes if you're involved in a minor traffic accident. Picture it, there you are, waiting at a roundabout, searching for a gap, when...BANG. You've been *rear-ended*. Nightmare. But, try not to panic. Breathe. Then get out. Take photos. Take a name, an address and a phone number. Take a note of any damage. But don't expect any help from your Examiner. Your test isn't over. Dealing with the situation is still all down to you.

All sorted? So, how are you feeling? How's your Examiner feeling? How's your car? Lights still working? Well, if everyone and everything's okay, and you've got enough detail to accurately report the crash to your insurance company, you can leave the scene of the bump and continue with your test. After all, you didn't do anything wrong, so you haven't failed. But again, remember, chances are your Examiner won't help you. In this situation, there are stories of Examiners just sitting there, waiting to see if the candidate plans on continuing the test!

And nobody, in this situation, would blame you for giving up. I certainly wouldn't. But maybe you're made of sterner stuff. Maybe you're determined to see it through.

Anyway, as I've said, observing you on your drive, and making a note of any mistakes, is one part of an Examiner's job. But there's another aspect to his job that concerns us, and that's that he also directs you around your test route. So, next we're going to cover...

Route Directions

At the beginning of your test, once you've answered the safety question and got yourself settled into your car, your Examiner starts the drive by saying something like: 'I'd like you to follow the road ahead, unless road markings or traffic signs direct you otherwise. If I want you to turn left or right I'll tell you in good time.' Then he'll ask you if you understand, to which, hopefully, you'll say yes, then he'll tell you to, 'Move on when you're ready.'

So, what your Examiner has told you is that at any given junction, if he stays quiet, it's because he wants you to follow the road ahead. The exception to this are roundabouts. At roundabouts he'll always direct you. But at other junctions, including traffic-lights, if he wants you to follow the road ahead, he simply remains silent.

Following the road ahead sounds straightforward. But, although we drive on the left in the UK, it isn't always the left-hand lane that goes straight-ahead. No, sometimes arrows tell you to use

the centre or the right-hand lane. And, in traffic, usually you just follow the car in front. But not always. Sometimes you have to leave the safety of the queue and go your own way. So, following the road ahead isn't always as easy as it sounds. It requires awareness and planning. Your Examiner's not going to tell you which lanes to use. You're expected to sort out lanes and junctions for yourself.

So, to work on that, when you're out driving with your Supervisor, it's really important to practice following the road ahead. It's really important to get your Supervisor to occasionally *shut up* and let you sort out the lanes at complex junctions yourself. Because, on test, faced with a silent Examiner, you're going to struggle if you're used to your Supervisor constantly directing you.

Something else you'll need to practice for your test is called...

Independent Driving

What happens, at the start of your independent drive, is that your Examiner either asks you to start following direction signs for somewhere in particular, or he might set up his sat-nav and ask you to start following the directions that it gives you.

Whichever he chooses, this part of your test, the independent drive, lasts for about twenty minutes, so roughly half of the time you're out driving.

Now, the two main things to note about the independent drive are that, number one, if at any time you're unsure of where you should be going, or of what the sat-nav's telling you, then you can ask for clarification from your Examiner. You're not penalised for losing track of directions. But, as our American friends might say, try to ask for help *ahead of time*. So, approaching a roundabout, for example, if you don't know where to go, try to ask before you get there.

And, number two. If you do make a mistake, so if you find yourself in the wrong lane at a roundabout, or you realise that you're in the process of turning left when you should've turned right... well, again, try not to panic. Because provided you stay calm and stay safe you won't be marked down. All that'll happen is either your Examiner or the sat-nav will re-direct you back onto the correct route.

But, whatever you do, in that situation, don't try to make last-ditch lane-changes or turns. That would be potentially danger-ous. So that would be a fail. But you won't be failed for simply having a bad sense of direction!

Now, on your independent drive, if you're using the sat-nav, don't rely on it to tell you either your speed or what the current speed limit is. By all means, glance at the sat-nav's screen occa-sionally to check for upcoming junctions or turns, but still use your speedo to check your speed.

At the end of the independent drive, your Examiner will say, 'That's the end of your independent drive. From here I'll just dir-ect you as normal.' And then, true to his word, he'll start direct-ing you junction-by-junction again. Though, of course, he'll stay quiet if he just wants you to follow the road ahead.

So, to recap, over the course of your driving test, you'll most likely do:

- An eyesight test
- Two safety questions
- 20 minutes of independent driving
- A reversing manoeuvre
- A hill-start
- An angled start
- An emergency stop

Your Examiner might not get you to do everything on that list, but it's best to be prepared, just in case. But, whatever you're asked to do, soon enough you'll be back at the test centre, car parked, engine off, and your Examiner will turn to you and de-liver...

The Result

Yay! You've passed! Your Examiner gives you a quick run-down on where you could improve your driving. Then he asks you for your licence so that he can arrange for your full licence to be posted out to you. Now, if for some reason you'd prefer to hold on to your licence for a while, that's fine. But then you've got just two years to update it yourself. Two years? Sounds like ages. Well join the list of guys who've messed up and forgotten! They've had to re-sit both the theory and practical tests, and do the lot, all over again.

So, unless you have a *really* good reason not to, give the nice man your provisional licence straight away.

And now you can drive anywhere. You can drive on the motorways. You can drive at night, drive in the rain, take passengers... the world is your oyster. But, today is now the first day of your two year probation period. Two years. And if you get six penalty points within those two years then your licence is *revoked*. That

means torn up. Now, you're not actually banned, so theoretically you can still drive...just as soon as you've done your theory test and driving test all over again. Yep, you have to start from scratch. Nightmare.

And six points *isn't* six offences. Speeding offences, say, aren't one point each! No, most offences carry a three point penalty. Some will even get you the six points all in one go. But don't panic, there isn't a police constable waiting for you on every street corner. But if you start to take chances...well, there's a fair chance you'll be joining those thousands of new drivers who, every year, have their licences revoked.

So that's if you pass. But what if you fail? Well, first of all, commiserations. But don't be put off. Listen carefully to your Examiner's feedback. Apply for another test, get lots more driving practice, and pass next time.

LESSON 19:
MOCK TESTS

The idea of mock testing is for your Supervisor to take a step back from instructing you for a while, and to announce, *I'm not going to instruct you here unless it's to avoid a potentially dangerous situation.*

Start off with a mix of about a dozen junctions that'll take around ten minutes to drive around, in an area that you both know reasonably well. Do the first lap as normal, your Supervisor offering advice and instruction as he sees fit. But then do another lap, this time with your Supervisor merely directing you. *At the end of the road, turn left.* That kind of thing.

Your Supervisor needs to take notes as you go. Trying to remember particular junctions doesn't work. Here, amongst other things, we're looking at your:

- Use of mirrors and blind spot checks
- Car control
- Timing and use of signals
- Road positioning
- Approach speeds
- Choice of gears
- Giving way where necessary
- Acceleration and use of speed

Your Supervisor starts with a blank sheet of paper and makes a quick note of any mistakes he sees. Then, afterwards, the two of you discuss those mistakes before you do a final lap, correcting the mistakes as you go.

Do a few different routes. The goal is to get you used to driving on your own, to get you used to the idea that your Examiner – on your actual test – won't step in to help you when the going gets tough.

Then move onto tackling a route that takes in a few more complex junctions, a couple of roundabouts and a few sets of traffic lights, a route that'll take fifteen-to-twenty minutes, and follow the same procedure:

- Warm up lap
- Mock test
- Corrections

And again, try a couple of different routes. Even doing a lap one way then simply turning around to tackle the same junctions in the opposite direction works just fine. That way you'll get two routes out of one set of junctions.

Next, move onto independent driving, either using a sat-nav – the one on your phone's fine – or following signs. Same thing, start with ten minutes and build up.

Do the same thing with your manoeuvres. Do a couple with supervision to warm up then tackle one on your own, from start-to-finish, with no help.

Remember, the key to passing a driving test is to be able to drive unaided. If you need help from your Supervisor then you'll definitely get found out by your Examiner!

When you've built up, and done each of these exercises a few times, it's time to move onto a full mock test.

Your Supervisor needs to earn his stripes here, because he's going to have to work out a route that takes in a mix of roads and junction types, that allows for a twenty minute independent drive, and has suitable places for a hill-start, angled-start, emergency stop, and a reverse manoeuvre.

Try to take this seriously. No chatting. During the drive, ask your Supervisor to clarify anything you don't understand. Focus on your driving.

Now, you're going to make mistakes. But don't give up. Sort yourself out and carry on. Get round the route.

And don't be disheartened. Very few people pass a first mock test. Remember, your goal is to drive the route unaided, or at least, virtually unaided, then to get any mistakes you've made presented to you in black-n-white.

Finally, if you've made your way through all of our lessons on here, and only had driving practice with your Supervisor, without any formal lessons from an instructor, then, first of all, well done! But this might be the time to finally employ an Instructor to help you and your Supervisor out.

A professional Driving Instructor is called an ADI: Approved Driving Instructor. The approved part means that they've been through a tough three-part government testing process, as well as passing stringent background checks. They carry an official certificate.

Anyway, an instructor will be able to take you for a more realistic and rigorous mock test. An instructor will take you out of your comfort zone, put you through your paces, and look at your driving through fresh eyes. It'll also give you some experience of driving with a stranger in the car.

Anyway, if you choose to make use of an instructor, it should be money well spent. And it'll move you closer to your goal, closer to Lesson 20, our final lesson: Driving Test Day.

LESSON 20: TEST DAY AND REGIONAL TEST VARIATIONS

Like all exams, your driving test prep starts the day before. So if you're using your own car, give it a quick wash-n-vacuum, and clean the windows. Look round the tyres, check the lights, and make sure it has plenty of fuel. Oh, and remember to make sure you have a stick-on rear-view mirror, for your Examiner to use.

Get all your car's paperwork together, stick it in a nice fat envelope, and put it somewhere that will remind you to take it with you tomorrow. Then find your licence and theory test certificate, and stick them in the nice fat envelope too.

Do you wear glasses? Find them, give them a clean, and put them with your nice fat envelope. Organise your contacts, if you use those. Oh, and grab your sunglasses. Yes, of course you can wear them if it's sunny.

Then add a small bottle of water and a snack, in case you get thirsty or peckish.

Oh, and you'd be amazed how many people turn up for their test on the wrong date or at the wrong time! So check that now. Then check that your Supervisor or Instructor are all organised for the big day, and confirm times with them.

Then do some revision. Remember all that stuff that you called *theory*? Well tomorrow it changes from theory to *actual*. So, do you remember all the rules for pedestrian crossings? Zigzag lines and flashing amber lights? What about if a traffic light's not working?

So, take thirty minutes to read through your *Highway Code*. And maybe check back in with some of the lessons on here.

And give some thought to what you're going to wear tomorrow. Something comfy but not too warm. Something that makes you feel good without looking like you're going to a wedding. Sensible shoes.

Finally, plan for an early night, phone on charge but set to silent, and set your alarm. So, to recap, the day before:

- Double-check you've got the right time, date and test centre
- Confirm times with your Supervisor or Examiner
- Find your driving licence and theory test certificate
- Find any documents you might need for your car
- Water and snack
- Glasses, contacts or sunglasses
- Clean your car
- Mirror for your Examiner
- Check the tyres and lights
- Fuel
- Revise
- Clothes
- Charge your phone
- Set your alarm

On the day, give yourself plenty of time for the drive over to the test centre. Plan for enough time to do a couple of practice manoeuvres on your way over, just to get yourself up-to-speed.

Some people are absolutely fine on the drive over to the test centre. Others not so much! You may find you make lots of mistakes. Don't panic. That's pre-test nerves messing with your head. Some people drive really slowly on the way over, some go at it like a rally driver! Again, don't panic – this is all normal.

So, as I said, these are pre-test nerves. Like a school exam. When you turn over the exam paper and write your name, the nerves fade. And here, when you start the actual test, you'll be fine as well.

If you've been to the test centre before, arrive there around fifteen minutes before your test appointment. But if you've never had chance to visit and look around, allow yourself five minutes more, so twenty minutes. Remember, try not to get in the way of guys coming into the test centre at the end of their tests. So watch for 'L' drivers, especially those with passengers wearing fluorescent jackets! But also remember that not all tests are in 'L' cars.

Park your car so that you can drive forwards away from the space you've chosen. Have a chat with your Supervisor about possible manoeuvres you might be asked to do at the test centre. Talk about your route out of the centre, and also any possible routes you might use on the way back in. Try to picture the actual junctions and the lanes you'll use.

Then grab your stuff – including your glasses, if you wear them – and head over to the waiting room.

Five minutes to go. Take a drink of water. Use the bathroom. Have your licence and theory certificate ready for your Examiner.

Then your Examiner appears. There are smiles and introductions. He asks to see your licence and theory letter, and asks you to sign to confirm your car's legal. He asks you if you want your Supervisor to accompany you on test. Then he leads you outside, and over to the car park, where you'll do your eyesight test, before finally heading over to your nice clean car.

At the car, you'll possibly do one of your safety questions. Then you'll be invited to make yourself comfortable in the driver's seat, while your Examiner gives the car a quick once-over.

Now you're in, sitting comfortably – so no coats or scarves – seat-belt on, and your Examiner climbs into the passenger seat. If you haven't done your safety question yet, you'll be asked it now. There are more pleasantries. Your Examiner adjusts the mirror, the one you've stuck to the windscreen for him. Then he gives you a bit of test information…until, at long last, your Examiner starts the driving part of the test.

He says something like: *I'd like you to follow the road ahead unless signs or road markings indicate otherwise. If I want you to turn, I'll tell you in good time. Move on when you're ready, please.*

Okay, this is it. Control your breathing. Make sure the car's secure then start the engine. Into gear. Have a good look around. Are any other driving test candidates moving away at exactly the same time as you? If so, watch them carefully, they might be even more nervous than you are!

Finally, after all the weeks and months of practice, you're off. Remember, this test will fly by. You'll be on your way back in no time. Try to do the basics well: 50% of fails are a result of a mistake relating to mirrors, blind spot checks, or something to do with priority, especially at junctions.

Drive carefully, keeping things as smooth as possible. At junctions, allow yourself plenty of time, no sudden movements. Drive like a chauffeur, not like you're late for work! Remember, *your Examiner will be quick to fail you if you're too quick, but slow to fail you if you're too slow*. So take your time. There's no rush.

On the test you'll be doing:

- Another safety question

- An independent drive
- A reversing manoeuvre
- A hill-start
- An angled start
- An emergency stop

Not all tests do everything on that list, and there are also some regional variations for Wales and Northern Ireland. We'll go through those in a minute.

Anyway, eventually you'll be on your way back to the test centre, recognising the route home. Finally, you'll be back in a bay at the test centre, engine off. Then the moment of truth… The result!

Fingers crossed: you've passed. Usually your Examiner will now take your licence from you and arrange for a new one to be posted out. And he'll chat briefly about any driving faults you may have made. And then that's it. Job done.

But if you didn't pass this time…reapply. Then get lots more practice and pass it next time.

Now, as I said, the test I've been describing relates to the UK driving test. But there are some…

Regional Variations

…for both Wales and Northern Ireland.

In Wales, you get the chance to celebrate your own language, if you wish, by using a 'D' plate, rather than an 'L' plate, and you can also request for your test to be conducted in Welsh.

In Northern Ireland it's a bit more involved. The main difference is the speed limit. On roads with a speed limit of more than 40mph, learners, and drivers who've just passed their test, are restricted to forty-five. Also, Northern Ireland candidates are still asked both of their safety questions at the beginning of the test, and the independent driving is for a shorter period, and also, doesn't involve use of a sat-nav.

And, finally, as we discussed at length in Lesson 17, Northern Ireland candidates, for their reversing manoeuvre, may be asked to do a *turn in the road* or to *reverse into a side road*, also known as a *left hand reverse*. But they don't yet do *pulling over on the right-hand-side of the road*, or driving *forwards into a parking space*.

And that, folks, is the end of our final lesson. I hope you've found them informative and enjoyable. Remember this book is available as audio, or in a written word format as either an eBook or paperback. And also, if you've enjoyed it, and you haven't already done so, then please give it a lovely review! Good reviews are the lifeblood of independent authors.

Thank you for taking the time to read this book. I hope you go on to enjoy a lifetime of safe – but occasionally adventurous – driving. And if you'd like further reading or listening to help you on that journey, may I suggest another of my titles: ***Surviving After Your Driving Test***.

COVID-19

As you know, 2020 was – quite literally – plagued by a new type of coronavirus which can lead to a really nasty respiratory disease known as Covid-19. And since its arrival in the UK, and the subsequent three-month lockdown, Covid-19 has led to some changes to the driving test.

But, before getting onto the changes as they stand now – so as I'm writing this – first of all remember that things are changing all the time, and often rapidly, so keep an eye on your local media for the most up-to-date information. And I say *local* media for two reasons. First, because, all parts of the UK are subject to local differences; so Scotland's driving tests during this crisis are likely to be different from, say, England's. And second, the media, because, in all honesty, that's where the country's driving instructors are also getting the majority of their information from. The Government agencies charged with running the show don't place keeping driving instructors up to speed high on their to-do list!

Anyway, so what changes are you likely to face if you're taking a test during this period? The first is that often appointment times are being staggered to prevent too many people gathering together in the test centre waiting rooms. This one isn't a particular problem for you, though. In fact, it could be an advantage, as you're now less likely to have to deal with other learner drivers at the test centre, either at the beginning or end of your test. And you're also far less likely to suffer from the problems that can occur if two tests start at the same time and then end up doing the same test route. When this happens, you can potentially spend your entire driving test in a dance with the other learner, one of you leading the other!

At the test centre you may find that the toilet facilities aren't open to the public. So try not to get caught short! Vending machines, likewise, are likely to not be in use.

Also your first meeting with your Examiner is likely to be held outside, with you then being taken into a covered area for your documentation to be checked. Also, any initial briefing that you might get from your Examiner will probably be conducted outside, so before you get nice-n-comfy in your car.

For the test, you'll need to wear a mask, unless you have a medical reason to not do so, and in that case, you must state this when booking the test, not on the day of the test. And your Instructor or Supervisor isn't likely to be able to accompany you out on the test, unless they're acting as an interpreter.

Then, on the test itself, the main difference in relation to the marking of the test is that if your Examiner decides that you have failed, he will cut your time short, and direct you straight back to the test centre. So if, say, you were to fail in the first few minutes, then you'd find yourself back in the test centre, possibly without even having done any of the manoeuvres that you've just spent the last few weeks perfecting.

If this does happen, your Examiner won't tell you that you've failed while you're driving. No, he'll simply continue the test in the normal way, but, as I said, direct you by the quickest route back to the test centre. Then he'll deliver the bad news to you once you're safely parked-up and your engine's switched off.

Now, a couple of points to think about. The first is that virtually everyone says that their test flew by. Honestly, I can't tell you how many pupils have told me that their test felt like it was over in minutes. Also, after a test, when I question a pupil on what route they were taken on, or what reversing manoeuvre they were asked to do, it's not unusual for them to not remember. *Haven't got a clue* is often how that conversation ends!

So, if you do realise that you're on your way back to the test centre, and it feels like you're being taken back early, don't panic – there's a good chance you've been out a lot longer, and done a lot more, than you realise.

And finally, remember that your Examiner might be intending for you to finish the test by reversing into a parking bay back at the test centre. So, so-what if you're heading back but you haven't done a manoeuvre yet. That doesn't mean you've failed.

Remember the mantra: Don't give up!

ABOUT THE AUTHOR

Mark Johnston

Mark's first word was 'car'. But his road experience got off to a bad start - 'run over' three times on the streets of London, all before the age of eight!

Since then Mark's helped literally thousands of people to pass their driving tests in England and Northern Ireland, and in 2015 received the Northern Ireland Driving Instructor of the Year award.

He now lives with his wife and family in a windswept Irish farmhouse.

BOOKS IN THIS SERIES

Learn to Drive UK

Everything you need to get you through your driving test and beyond. In paperback, eBook and Audio.

Teach Yourself To Drive In 20 Lessons

The 20 Lessons every profesional driving instructor will take you through.

Surviving After Your Driving Test

Shift your driving up a gear! Everything your 'L' test lessons didn't get round to teaching you. A generation of driving experience in one book.

Learning To Drive Journal

A place to keep all your driving related notes. Part diary, part notebook, part keepsake.

My Driving Notebook

A place to keep all your driving related notes. Part diary, part notebook, part keepsake.

My Driving Logbook

A place to keep all your driving related notes.

Printed in Great Britain
by Amazon